THE
ACCOMPLISHED
CREATIVE

THE
ACCOMPLISHED
CREATIVE

OVERCOME IMPOSTER SYNDROME, FORGE COURAGE, AND TAP INTO LIMITLESS CREATIVITY

JEREMY RICHARDS

Published by Best Seller Publishing®, St. Augustine, FL
Best Seller Publishing® is a registered trademark.
Printed in the United States of America.

ISBN: 978-1-959840-33-6

For more information, please write:
Best Seller Publishing®
53 Marine Street
St. Augustine, FL 32084
or call 1 (626) 765-9750
Visit us online at: www.BestSellerPublishing.org

Contents

INTRODUCTION.. XI

The History of This "Imposter".................................. xii

What We're Doing Here xiv

The Commitment to Change xx

Reversing the Forgetting Curve xxii

Don't Throw Your Kindle Across the Room............... xxv

1   YOU'RE JUST PRETENDING TO HAVE IMPOSTER SYNDROME......1

Impersonating Imposter Syndrome 4

Pobody's Nerfect 5

Your Inner Critic is the Real Imposter..........................9

It's Not Your Default..11

Stop Faking It and Start Making It................................15

I Bet This Roller Coaster Only Goes Up! 19

Minimum Viable Practice: What's the Point? 24

Whoa There! (Overdoing It)..25

The Balancing Act...27

2   THE UNSTOPPABLE ARTIST—INSPIRATION AND INFLUENCE..... 31

Courage, Skill, and Inspiration: CSI 32

The Imposter Inventory...38

Breathe It In 47

Minimum Viable Practice: The Morning Pages...........49

Overdoing it: Inspiration as Cliché 50

The Balancing Act: Stepping out of the Crowd 54

3   BUILDING THE PLANE IN MID-AIR—HOW TO THINK LIKE

    AN IMPROVISER...**55**

    Working it Out 57

    The Improvising Imposter...59

    Your Brain on Improv 63

    Getting Into Flow 66

    What are You Doing? 69

    Association Flow...73

    Gratitude Flow 75

    Minimum Viable Practice: I Notice, I Wonder, What If...............78

    Whoa There: Overthinking and Underdoing or Overdoing and

    Underthinking? 80

    Balancing Act: Second Naïveté 81

4   NAKED IN A STRANGER'S DINING ROOM—MEDITATION,

    MINDFULNESS, AND THE IMPERFECT PATH **85**

    The Imperfect Path 88

    Minimum Viable Practice: Sit down, Be Humble 90

    Whoa There: Climbing Back Out of Your Mind............................93

    Balancing Act: RAIN and Loving Kindness.................................96

    Recognize, Allow, Investigate, Nurture 98

    Kindness: I'm Loving It.. 100

5   HEMLOCK AND KEY—LET'S MAKE OUR BRAINS HURT

    WITH SOME PHILOSOPHY..**103**

    Philosophy as Counterweight.. 108

    A Philosophical Tasting Menu.. 111

    Minimum Viable Practice: Question Your Inner Guard 121

    Whoa There: Flapping Your Arms 123

    The Balancing Act: Fiercely Practical 126

6   FIND YOUR TRIBE—CREATING THROUGH COMMUNITY 129
    Creative Community Vibe Checklist 133
    The Resonance Era 134
    Minimum Viable Practice: The Audience Window 136
    Whoa There: The Thirsty Creative 141
    Balancing Act: Between Hiding and Exploiting 143

7   A STUPID WALK FOR YOUR STUPID MENTAL HEALTH 147
    The Whole House Shakes 150
    Whoa There: One Good Left Hook 154
    Balancing Act: Cuddle and Tap 155

8   TODAY'S THE DAY! UNLESS YESTERDAY WAS THE
    DAY, THEN PRETEND IT'S TOMORROW BUT TODAY IS
    YESTERDAY. TODAY IS... A DAY! 157
    Oprah Opens the Box 159
    No Puppies Were Harmed 163
    Time After Timeboxing 166
    Your Infinite Parallel Days 167

ACKNOWLEDGMENTS 181
ABOUT THE AUTHOR 183
REFERENCES 185
ENDNOTES 191

Let's face it, if you're alive, stay out of art. If you're
a nice person with good self-esteem and you see a
camera, a pencil, or a paintbrush coming your way,
run like hell. It's history coming to mug you.
–Andrei Codrescu

The universe is an arrow
without end and it asks only one question:
How dare you?
–Paige Lewis

These mountains that you are carrying,
you were only supposed to climb.
–Najwa Zebian

Introduction

When I told my friends I was writing a book about imposter syndrome, one of them quipped, "Are you sure you're qualified?"

Jokes aside, they had a point: I'm not a psychologist, guru, or the vessel of a centuries-old spiritual being who has chosen me to channel arcane wisdom through a creepy and problematic voice. Beyond that, I wasn't sure if my experience of imposter syndrome was convincing enough to relate to anyone seriously grappling with self-doubt. Sure, I grew up a poor, sickly, outcast; a gangly bully magnet with a chipped front tooth (frozen Toblerone) fumbling through career choices well into my 30s, and still sometimes seized with doubts even on my best days. But despite that loser litany, let's be real: I'm still a white guy born in the United States with a couple of college degrees and (not to brag) a copy of Plato's *Republic* signed by They Might Be Giants.[1] I am constantly unpacking my privilege and then repacking my privilege with all the grace of folding a fitted sheet and stuffing

---

[1]   Kudos to the three TMBG fans who got that reference.

it into a shoebox–my fractured upbringing and social awkwardness act as decent counterweights to inherited entitlement.

THE HISTORY OF THIS "IMPOSTER"

At age 14, following my parents' divorce, my father and I were living in the carpeted attic of a halfway house. Of the other 17 residents, 10 were recovering addicts, and four had recent return addresses at the state prison. An octogenarian nun named Helen[2] owned and ran the halfway house as part of her Christian mission to bring each wayward soul back into the fold, regardless of their sins, their history, or their tendency to stay up late blasting AC/DC and throwing empty Miller Lite cans out of the second-story window. After a few months, my dad and I "upgraded" from the attic to the second floor, to a room with a ceiling high enough to stand up straight, but which was half the stretch of the tattered attic. Meanwhile, I found a clean corner of the room to do my homework, watch Comedy Central on the stolen cable, and do my best to sleep. We mostly ignored the nightly riots.

Until we didn't. One night, my dad was fed up. He pounded on the door across the hall and told our ex-con neighbor with the meaty shoulders and burning skull neck tattoo that he needed to "quiet down or end up out on the street." This wasn't meant to be a threat—my dad had assumed a peaceful and diplomatic means for resolution—but our neighbor took it as a threat. He exploded through the door, pushing my dad back across the hall and into our room, screaming that he was seconds away from killing him.

---

[2]   Many names in this book have been changed
        to protect my imperfect memory.

My first thought? *Find my skateboard and start swinging. No, wait. Find my skateboard, hold it up, feint a swing, then kick him in the balls, and when he bends over in pain, THEN I crack the skateboard against his head.* But honestly, what was I going to do—me, with my question mark backbone and breadstick legs? Fortunately, I had left my skateboard downstairs. Fortunately, my dad whimpered and backed down. Our neighbor shook it off and went back to crank "Thunderstruck" to max volume.

As usual, I didn't sleep well that night. Even if we escaped that one threat, I realized that if something drastic didn't change, we would always be cowering, always feeling trapped. In the two or three hours of sleep I somehow managed to get that night, I crawled through nightmares of collapsing bridges and a piano made of broken bones.

The next morning, I got up with a new resolve. I went downstairs, retrieved my skateboard, and rode straight to the library. I was chasing a burning question, and figured there must be an answer somewhere there in the stacks: *Why do we do what we do?* By that I meant, *Why does anyone do anything? How can we change? Does it really have to be this way?* I piled up every book I could find on psychology, Western and Eastern philosophy, sociology, neuroscience... then, I eventually moved beyond linear approaches and started in on fiction, poetry, theater, and theories of art and creativity. Back in high school, I joined an improv class and started writing plays—explorations of dysfunctional human behavior disguised as surreal one-acts.

In the 30 years since that day, I've devoured hundreds of books swirling around these questions of motivation, behavior, and expression, eventually leading me to a career in coaching, consulting, and leadership development (basically explaining to corporate clients why they do what they do). In parallel, I've also followed my obsession with a creative life, ranging from photography and performance poetry to philosophical musi-cals and improvised Shakespeare. In the intersection between theory and creativity, I teach applied improv classes, helping teams hone their collaboration and tap into their instincts for innovation.

But it all started that night in the halfway house. I can draw a line from that 14-year-old kid cowering in the room to the life and career I have now—not a direct line, but a line. I'd also be lying if I said that kid wasn't still haunting me. The poet Sandra Cisneros once described every former version of herself as a coin rattling around in an empty bandage tin. For any of us, I would add, some coins are heavier than others, and over the years their currency shifts. Doubt creeps in. *What if, at my core, I'm still that scrawny, clueless kid, just dressing my wounds with big words and ornate metaphors? What if everything I've earned is just on loan and about to come due? What am I even doing here?*

Unless you somehow missed the title of this book and just started flipping through randomly, you can probably guess my answer.

WHAT WE'RE DOING HERE

Self-doubt and negative self-talk seldom feel under our control. With imposter syndrome, that critical little voice inside our heads targets our self-image specifically when we are in the process of achieving something in life. It makes us feel that we are not deserving of the identity and/or recognition that we get—or denies that we even deserve the credit.

The term imposter syndrome was first coined by psychol-ogists Suzanna Imes and Pauline Rose Clance in 1978 (conspiratorially, the year I was born). Imes and Clance originally called this thought and behavior pattern "imposter phenomenon," or the deep-seated feeling that one is a fake or one's behavior is fraudulent.[i] For those of us who have chosen an imaginative life, for us performers, artists, writers, and musicians, we find identity tied to expression, and expression tied to the ethereal, ineffable notion of "inspiration"—the shit we are just making up. Meanwhile, we see hard-working builders, doctors,[3] soldiers, and engineers flawlessly marching along the clear path set out for them, and we assume (often wrongly) that their identity, actions, education, and desires are easier to define than our own.

Often, within our own identities the split happens in our twin pursuits: the engineer/poet, oncologist/cellist, pilot/painter. We're stuck feeling that these diverging paths are contradictions instead of paired expressions of the same drive. Left unchecked, this rift leaves us at war with ourselves, facing what Steven Pressfield calls resistance, all coiled up in the energies of inner drama and draining our inherent source of expression.

Ski Jumps and Waterslides

> *This very moment, we can change our lives. There never was a moment, and never will be, when we are without the power to alter our destiny.*
> –Stephen Pressfield

Over the years, I've facilitated onboarding classes for thousands of new employees, ranging from fresh college grads to tenured senior leaders. Most, if they are honest, will confess that they

---

[3]   Incidentally, a 2022 study from Stanford Medicine found that imposter syndrome is more prevalent in doctors than in most other professions in the U.S.

feel overwhelmed at first, regardless of past accomplishments or current titles. The same holds true for my coaching clients who are facing creative blocks. My common refrains aren't original but they always resonate:

1. You're not alone
2. You're here for a reason

On the surface, these are platitudes. Later, you will witness my tirade against clichés and perhaps wonder if I'm a hypocrite. My response is that A) Yes, we're all a bit hypocritical; I hear it's good for your joints, and B) Any time I employ a cliché, it's meant as a Trojan Horse.[4] That is, I'm always oscillating between being the facilitator who wants to keep the message accessible and the philosopher who wants to deconstruct every assumption to rewire expectations.

Okay, so "you're not alone." The Hallmark interpretation is that you're always within reach of loved ones, if only remotely, or that you are always within the radiance of good vibes from the universe (possibly, but not guaranteed to include your cat). For our purposes, if you relate to the sense of imposter syndrome, "you're not alone" also carries the connotation of, "Yeah, join the club." Later, we'll share the statistics and celebrities in this imposter club that will make your isolation feel more commonplace. More intriguing to me, however, is the research that pulls us out of our solipsistic space and insists that our sense of self and even our thought patterns are not just cloistered neurons firing in the dark chambers of our skull. Rather, they are part of an extensive relationship between our thoughts, expressions, embodiment, environment, the reflections of others, and the

---

4   "I see what you did there." –Every sitcom sidekick from 2007

dynamics of all those interactions in concert. So, yeah. You're not alone.

You've likely heard that "you're here for a reason" in different contexts, and it can mean many things. You might believe in a calling or higher purpose, but this "reason" could also be purely practical. You're here in this job because a hiring manager saw your potential to address a need. You're here in this studio because a flood of color and feeling pulled you from your dreams and put a paintbrush in your hand. You're here on this stage because the club owner heard your demo, and track three feels like a slow dance on the fire escape so sweet that the flames just wait and watch. The point is that you have unique experience, a unique form of expression, and an outlet to share your work with others—chances are, there are people out there who need your art in this world.

If we want to play with semantics, you're not just here for a reason, you're here for an emotion. You're here for an experience, an advantage, and a way out. If you're here for cotton candy and easy answers, then sorry, you're in the wrong line (that line is long but fast moving and tends to be circular).

Yes, despite the warm hug of a title, I'll warn you now that this book is not fluffy self-help or a "think positive" and "manifest your dreams" guide, nor is it a dry research paper. There are no cheer squads, drill sergeants, or cheese sandwiches here (apologies, I was dictating this last sentence through Siri and my six-year-old just asked for a cheese sandwich; but I'm leaving that here because it's true that this book is in fact not a cheese sandwich). What it is, though, is a wired journey that combines philosophies, purposes, and practices, all designed to move you from theory to creation.

The movement is everything. What if I had called this book *The Accomplishing Creative*? Awkward, but more accurate, in that "accomplished" implies that you've arrived, you're established, and not only have you acquired laurels (whatever those are), but you are so posh that those laurels are strictly for resting upon. I'd never wish that complacency on you, so if at times this book feels restless, please understand that energy has a trajectory.

In the decades I've spent reading those hundreds of books on personal development, like you, I've recognized patterns, similarities, and clichés—none of which inspire true change. I'm not immune to the occasional easy read for a sugar-rush of motivation, but whenever I feel glib or overconfident, I seek out dense philosophy and surreal poetry, something to pull me out of complacency and leave me happily baffled. After all, who needs rhyming self-help slogans when you can get this gem from Arundhati Roy:

"Another world is not only possible, she is on her way. On a quiet day, I can hear her breathing."

See? Happily baffled! I immediately feel what Roy means, but I'm not about to explain it away, let alone slap it on a bumper sticker and ask you to parse the metaphysics of hope while going 70 mph down I-5.

What wakes me up are the authors like Audre Lorde, David Whyte, bell hooks, or Julia Cameron—those who talk about human behavior with startling and poetic language. More than novelty, this approach holds more traction for our easily-distracted brains. In the journal *Frontiers*, neuroscientist Arthur M. Jacobs describes neurocognitive poetics as a keen strategy for hooking our attention and persisting in our memory:

> Poetic language plays with our affective and cognitive apparatus in a way that facilitates empirical investigation: it works with a catalog of formal stylistic devices and "figures of thought"

(e.g., polysemy, irony, meiosis, oxymoron) which reflect partially innate perceptual, affective, and cognitive schemata and allow clear predictions about how (and where in the brain) such verbal stimuli are processed, for instance in analogy to stimuli producing visual illusions (Schrott and Jacobs, 2011), or basic emotions (Jacobs et al., 2015), thus "presenting to us an experience perfectly designed for the human brain" (Turner and Pöeppel, 1983).[ii]

While I'll try (and sometimes fail) to resist being too twee or pretentious, the language of this conversation is deliberate. I treat poetic license like a fishing license—an excuse to escape and a justification for catching too much. As you're reading, if you find yourself confused, lost, disoriented, or a little hungry, then that's a sign that it's working. Some books on personal development are like an automated sidewalk at the airport–you just step on and it carries you along. This book isn't an automated sidewalk. It's a steep climb through an alpine forest that sometimes reverses course with ski jumps and waterslides. This book is designed to interrupt your patterns and slingshot you out of your comfort zone.

THE COMMITMENT TO CHANGE

> *What saves you is to take a step. Then another step.*
> *It is always the same step, but you have to take it.*
> –Antoine de Saint-Exupéry

As a catalyst for change, this book is also about finding a balance and a healthy tension between extremes—between structure and freedom, confidence and humility, and expression and introspection. You'll notice that each chapter has sections that adjust the throttle between polar expressions:

Minimum Viable Practice (MVP)

You start with a step. Establish a test before a habit. No one is grading you here, so practice self-compassion. If any recommended practice seems off or too unwieldy at first, you can set it aside for now, but this MVP approach will give you a low-risk entry point.

Whoa There (aka Overdoing It)

With any new practice, artists especially can become infatuated and over-committed. For each core practice in a chapter, I'll cite the research and share the personal scars that shape the border of these extremes. Your mileage may vary,[5] so listen to your body, stay mindful, and consult your doctors, mental health practitioners, Instagram life coaches, etc.

---

[5]   Do Canadians say *your kilometrage may vary*?

The Balancing Act

To paraphrase Acharya Rajneesh, the term "finding balance" betrays the nature of true balance, which we experience as a verb, not a noun. You're never statically in balance; rather, you are always approaching or retreating, moving toward or away, and at times, in the space of a breath, feeling weightless in equilibrium. Don't get too comfortable. We'll continue to return to this last aspiration of the balancing act as an ongoing pursuit.

To throw back another curtain on the strategy of this book, I'm also applying the lessons I learned from my decades of experience in learning and development to help the theories presented here translate into practice. Call it wonky, but I'm convinced that giving you a dose of the learning theory will make your journey toward courageous creativity more potent and applicable.

If you're struggling with imposter syndrome and identifying an authentic sense of self, you need to reflect on your memories and how you assemble these into a cohesive persona for yourself. If you're going to change, you must begin with reflection influenced by experience and intentional learning. But identity is memory, and memory is fallible. Consider the prevalent science fiction narrative of implanted memories defining or redefining a whole being, from *Blade Runner* to *Battlestar Galactica* to *Westworld*. Who would you be within someone else's narrative? Meanwhile, how often do you find yourself making the same mistakes and circling the same ruts, no matter how much you think you've learned?

REVERSING THE FORGETTING CURVE

> *I witness with pleasure the supreme achievement*
> *of memory, which is the masterly use it makes of*

innate harmonies when gathering to its fold the
suspended and wandering tonalities of the past.
—Vladimir Nabokov

For our purposes, memory plays a dual role, stretching backwards and forwards—from what we retrieve to what we retain. When I share glimpses of my past, I'm nudging your own backup hard drive to start whirring, to summon the forgotten files and archived registries that hold clues about your current operating system. Moving forward, then, when I conjure weird literary tactics and obscure humor, I'm following a neuroscience-based tactic to make these lessons last.

This likely isn't the first book you've read on personal development, nor is it likely to be the last. Consider those books that inspired you the most, that you bookmarked and dog-eared and streaked with yellow highlights—how much of that wisdom have you retained? How much have you applied?

In my profession of leadership development, we often battle against *The Forgetting Curve*—a phenomenon first formally documented in 1885 by Hermann Ebbinghaus[iii] (hence the saying, "I totally Ebbinghaused where I left my keys"). There are many factors influencing retention, but in short, the research (also replicated in 2015[iv]) tells us that we forget half of what we learn within a matter of days. Without spaced repetition, all of those compelling facts, concepts, and stories might atrophy to 10% or less of what you originally learned.

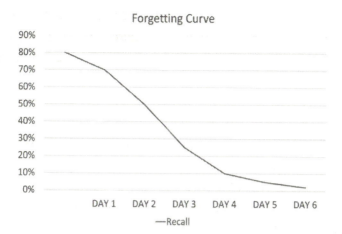

In my corporate roles, I owned learning programs that cost companies millions in development and deployment, so the stakes were high to combat The Forgetting Curve and drive retention and application.

As cognitive neuroscientist Dr. Caroline Leaf observes, when we constantly accumulate knowledge without applying it, all of the books and courses and podcasts at 2x speed will do nothing but contribute to our analysis paralysis–a dizzying overwhelm with no clue where to start. Even the knowledge we forget feels like it's building up a bloat of unresolved needs.

What can we do to mitigate The Forgetting Curve? As noted, the most obvious route is spaced repetition over the days and weeks after learning. That said, for topics related to human behavior, where the goal goes beyond recounting facts, true application requires more than brute-force study sessions.

Habits and mindset are like good posture. One morning you skim over an article about raising your chest and tucking your chin, and suddenly you're strutting in full superhero mode. But eventually fatigue sets in, and before you know it, you're back to trudging along like Moe Sizlack, the sad sack bartender from *The Simpsons*.

The same pattern might hold for your courage, your persistence, or your inspiration. Here's the reality: No matter how much you know about the habit you're trying to instill, you won't truly change until you build the right postural muscles and condition the proper flexibility and mobility—until your new approach is fully embodied. (We'll dive more into literal embodiment in Chapter 7.) How difficult is it to remember to stand up straight? Yet how easy is it to slouch? You don't just need more information or more encouragement. You need that constant reminder, humming along until it colonizes your basal ganglia on the level of pure instinct.

Here are some of my go-to's for boosting retention and the application of learning:

1. Strategically-spaced repetition with an app like Readwise.
2. Cross-referencing new material with older sources on the same topic.
3. Teaching the content back to others through instructional design, facilitation, and writing. For you, this might be more casual, such as conversations with friends and family, posts on social media, or incorporating the insights into your own work or teaching.

PUT IT INTO PRACTICE

What are your approaches to recalling and applying what you learn, especially for content designed to influence your behavior?

DON'T THROW YOUR KINDLE ACROSS THE ROOM

> *When you have exhausted all possibilities,*
> *remember this: you haven't.*
> –Thomas Edison

Overcoming imposter syndrome is not just about what you are learning or creating, but about *who you are becoming*. By the end of each approaching chapter, you might feel restless. This book is designed to get you off the couch, bean bag, or ergonomic unicycle you use for reading—beyond contemplation and into action. I envision you opening the blinds, lacing up your running shoes, or grabbing the nearest pen/paintbrush/camera/oboe and embodying the courage to create. If you throw this book across the room out of sheer inspiration and not frustration, I'll know it's doing its job.

In the coming chapters, we'll also take some turns that will feel, at first, like detours. But, once you follow the shape of each chapter, you will see how they each attack imposter syndrome from a different angle (if only to poke it with a sharp stick and run away). As we track these different approaches to mindset, behavior, and performance, each step will take time to settle in, and you will get out of it what you put into it. (For example, if you put pickles into this book, you get pickles out of it. That's an odd choice on your part, but don't say I didn't warn you.) On the other hand, if you put in the practice, answer the prompts, apply the lessons to your own circumstances, admit where you agree or disagree with me, then all your effort will compound into something more meaningful than a casual read. There's nothing casual about this book—unless, of course, you just want something casual right now and you're not looking for something serious. I mean, no expectations here, cool, yeah, we can keep it super casual and... you know, just see where it goes.

Chapter 1
You're Just Pretending to Have Imposter Syndrome

The curious paradox is that when I accept
myself just as I am, then I can change.
–Carl Rogers

I wish I could show you when you are lonely or in
darkness the astonishing light of your own being.
–Hafiz

A woman lies unconscious on a conference table. As she wakes, dazed, she hears a disembodied voice crackle over the intercom:

"Who are you?"

Like many of us, she doesn't know how to answer that question. In this case, the woman literally does not know who she is, where she is, where she was born, or the color of her mother's eyes. Aside from a retention of basic skills and language, she is a blank slate. *Lost, then, or liberated?* That's the operative question that keeps us hooked.

If you're a fan of prestige television, you likely recognize the opening scene of *Severance*, Dan Erickson's darkly funny and philosophical series that debuted in 2022. If you're not familiar with the show (or if you inhabit a severed consciousness not allowed to watch TV), I'll try to bring you up to speed. In the world of *Severance*, an Orwellian corporation has developed the technology to "sever" the memories of certain employees so that they have no memory of their life before the procedure—at least while in the confines of certain company property. In this way, they develop "innie" personalities who know nothing but their 9-to-5 reality, while their "outies" have no knowledge or memory of what they do while at work. (You know what? Just go watch the first season. I'll wait.)

As countless online thinkpieces and podcasts about *Severance* will attest, we are all "severed" to some degree. We show up, smile, "leave our issues at the door," and to varying degrees, turn our inward dials up or down to meet the expectations of our roles. From what I've researched, what coaching clients have confided, and my own experience, this fluidity of self-presentation is normal.[6]

We then see a shift from the subtle inflections of daily adjustments to the major, *Doctor-Who*-Regeneration-level of reinvention during major life transitions. Graduation, marriage, a new career, becoming a parent, divorce—each a rite of passage that recasts us in our own roles.

As Mel Robbins put it, "Every phase of your life and career will require a different you."

That Robbins quote is an absolute mic drop for imposter syndrome. If you could fully process and internalize that right now, I'd pack it up and let you leave this book early to beat

---

[6]   Yes, you in the back of the room with your hand up? Oh, what about Multiple/Dissociative Personality Disorder? Well, first, you're in the wrong classroom. Also, that's a serious mental health condition affecting about 1% of the population, and as you might guess, it's outside of the scope of this book.

traffic. The challenge, of course, is that this realization and acceptance of a "different you" (or *yous*), is just the beginning of your journey. The question remains: *Who do you think you are?*

No one can diagnose you with imposter syndrome because it is not a diagnosis. It is a hazy label for a constellation of self-doubt, uncertainty, shame, and the stomach-swarm of existential vertigo. It's also surprisingly common. In her excellent book *The Imposter Cure*, clinical psychologist Dr. Jessamy Hibbard says that imposter syndrome:

> May appear as insecurity, self-doubt, fear of failure and perfectionism. Or as self-criticism, low self-esteem, an inability to accept compliments, or a focus on where you're falling short. It's a guard against arrogance and a safety net in case everything goes wrong. This list, rather than being titled '*Imposter Syndrome,*' could be titled '*The Problems of Being Human.*'

In a 2011 compilation of "imposter phenomenon" research, Jaruwan Sakulku and James Alexander estimate that 70% of people admit to feeling like imposters at some point in their lives.[v] Meanwhile, a 2020 study found that 84% of entrepreneurs struggle at times with feeling inadequate or inauthentic, also affirming the label of imposter syndrome.[vi] The term "at times" is operative here, as confidence may drop and surge; and as we'll see, a certain amount of doubt may be healthy.

Meanwhile, what are the other 16-30% of the adult population doing? Either they've transcended the human instinct for self-doubt, they misunderstood the survey question, or they've been replaced by an alien pod person who simply accepts their imposter status as a given. Oh, to have the equanimity of a pod person!

IMPERSONATING IMPOSTER SYNDROME

When a term like "imposter syndrome" catches on, it can be helpful for some, but a complete misdirect for others. Researcher and professor Dr. Mike Mena notes that "imposter phenomenon," as it was first coined, allowed for more complex external factors; whereas "imposter syndrome" redirects our attention to the individual subject, implying that there is something inherently wrong with your perception.[vii]

For people of color and other traditionally marginalized groups, Dr. Mena observes, there are countless systemic issues that could account for a lack of confidence, a muted expression, or a sense of being out of place. He sees the term more accurately described as *imposter training*. Researchers Ruchika Tulshyan and Jodi-Ann Burey make a similar point in their 2021 article for the *Harvard Business Review*, "Stop Telling Women They Have Imposter Syndrome:"

> Imposter syndrome is especially prevalent in biased, toxic cultures that value individualism and overwork. Yet the "fix women's imposter syndrome" narrative has persisted, decade after decade. We see inclusive workplaces as a multivitamin that can ensure that women of color can thrive. Rather than focus on fixing imposter syndrome, professionals whose identities have been marginalized and discriminated against must experience a cultural shift writ large.[viii]

Mena, Tulshyan, and Burey all have more depth and credibility on this front, and I aspire to be an ally. With my graduate work in cultural studies firmly aligned with feminism, anti-racism, and queer theory, I won't shy away from the cultural politics at play.

I will also make the case that we consider *both* the individual struggles and the cultural forces, and academic background aside, I'm more equipped to address the individual dimensions. I encourage you to explore the work of these scholars to supplement what you find here, as well as the groundbreaking work on White Supremacy Culture by Tema Okun, Ibram X. Kendi, and Layla Saad.

Meanwhile, if someone of authority gave you this "imposter syndrome" label as a reductionist view of all of your doubts and inhibitions, my hope is that this book will give you the perspectives, narratives, and tools to dismantle both individual and systemic assumptions and define your own identity from a more authentic source.

POBODY'S NERFECT

> *I am not who you think I am; I am not who I think*
> *I am; I am who I think you think I am.*
> –Charles Horton Cooley

Imposter syndrome is a disconnect between who you think you are and who you think you should be–between your perceived self and your ideal self. But those are not the only two options. Before we explore the alternative, here is what your perceived self and your ideal self have in common: they are both illusions.

When your inner criticism takes charge, your perceived self is limited, a failure, a fraud–according to that distorted view.

Meanwhile, your ideal self is perfect, productive, bulletproof, always confident and in control. But here's the thing: The part of you painting this picture of your ideal self is just your perfectionism in a wig and glasses.

"The greater the emphasis on perfection, the further it recedes" says the 16th century poet Swami Haridas. I would add that perfectionism doesn't raise your standards—it lowers your expectations. Again, that's the trick we keep falling for with the humble brag, "Ugh, I'm such a perfectionist." When you cast your standards to that receding horizon, you always fall short, covertly giving yourself an out because a deeper part of you knows you're chasing after the impossible. You've likely heard the bromide that "the perfect is the enemy of the good." As you internalize this battle, you find that the worst kind of enemy is the one you've conjured in your mind.

Here's the part of the infomercial that insists, *There's got to be a better way!*

But wait, there's more. In his book *The Pursuit of Perfect*, Psychologist and philosopher Tal Ben Shahar introduces the concept of *optimalism*. While *optimal* comes from the Latin *optimus*, meaning *best*, in Shahar's perspective, this "best" is still tethered to reality.

Your optimal self is:

- Present but not complacent
- Striving but accepting
- Imperfect but improving
- Content but still driven

As opposed to your mythical "ideal" or "perfect" self, your optimal self tries and fails and sometimes takes a spinning heel kick to the chin, but bounces right off that canvas and persists, because being your optimal self means you're doing your best. You're not perfect, but you're doing your best. So now: What are you going to do with it?

Here's a more systematic breakdown with my summation of Tal Ben Shahar's concepts:

Perfectionism	Optimalism
There is only one way to approach a problem or a situation. The path is linear.	The path is irregular—a spiral synthesis of everything life has to offer.
Failure is not an option.	Failure is an opportunity to learn and adapt.
Fixated on results.	Process-focused.
"All or nothing" approach.	Finding the "middle way," balanced.
Self-image is dependent on others; you get defensive about external appraisal.	You are open to suggestions and inputs when they come from well-intentioned and trusted sources.
Focusing on the flaws.	Recognizing areas of improvement but seeing the whole picture, including the highlights.
You are a harsh critic of yourself and others.	You start with self-reflection. You hold others accountable while remaining fair and open to understanding.

Perfectionism and optimalism both spring from the same necessity. The lens of each worldview makes the difference—refracting a fear of failure, for example, through the doom of perfectionism or the grounded preparation of optimalism. With optimalism, you also mitigate toxic positivity because you see negative outcomes and risks with a clear-eyed determination. If you fixate on "attracting only positive outcomes from the universe," or whatever, you succumb to the premise of *thought crimes*—that your unmonitored but natural fears can somehow manifest your dire fate.

Here's another truism that rhymes: *What you resist persists*. The tightly-wound avoidance of reality amplifies any fixation or neurosis you're trying to escape. A 2013 study in *PLoS ONE* found that, "Intrusive thoughts and attempts to suppress them are common, but while suppression may be effective in the short-term, it can increase thought recurrence in the long-term."[ix] (We'll explore better mechanisms for navigating our thoughts in Chapter 4.) For now, it's worth taking note of these knee-jerk assumptions from your inner voice, tying those assumptions to a chair, and interrogating them until they break down:

Artist's Myth	Reality
My story/vision/voice is not worth sharing.	How are you defining "worth?"
My past success was a fluke.	If you have succeeded in the past, you've already disproven your doubts. If anything, you have more experience, more insight, and more of an established audience than you did before.

I'm out of cold brew coffee. I can't create until I get more cold brew.	You have another jar of cold brew in the back of the fridge. No, it's... it's behind the salsa. There, see?

YOUR INNER CRITIC IS THE REAL IMPOSTER

The mind creates the abyss, and the heart crosses it.
–Sri Nisargadatta

In your inner employment office, why is the critic always the first and only hire? Further back in line you'll also find an inner champion, an inner river guide, an inner referee, and an inner jester. It's like a sitcom in there, and there's a whole season of antics you might be missing. If you're the showrunner in this scenario, you have more power than you realize, and you can hire, fire, or recast your show at any time.

When it comes to imposter syndrome, there is no such thing as an inner monologue; there is only an *inner dialogue*. The question then becomes, whose side are you on? Friedrich Nietzsche spoke of this internal voice as the call from their higher self. He wrote, "They (people in general) fear their higher self because when it speaks, it speaks demandingly," and their demands are often encrypted in hurtful words that puncture your fragile ego. The next time you listen to your inner voice while it criticizes you, try to see the wound beneath the complaint; it might even be unaddressed trauma that needs your attention.

Up until this point, I've been adopting the term "inner critic" because it was historically the popular conception of internalized doubt. But after poring over the research and working with over a hundred coaching clients over the past few years, I've found that this mental model is no longer useful. "Inner critic" conjures some position of expertise and credentials, but in reality, this element of your internal dialogue is limited by fear and negativity, blinding it to possibilities. Some use the term "inner enemy," urging you to "go to war with it," and building up stories of an almost supernatural force that's hellbent on dragging you into the underworld of anxiety and depression. That "inner enemy" narrative also feels like it's promoting more inner turmoil, because whatever you internalized is still a part of you. The combativeness is also likely to make you overcorrect with toxic positivity, dysregulating your complex emotions, and not giving your feelings a safe place to surface. Though I joked about the harsh interrogation of destructive thoughts, ultimately I disagree with the notion that you should go to war with this inner voice. Consider your interface with your doubts like an empathetic debate with a trusted friend—contemporary neuroscience tells us that pushing back stubbornly won't persuade anyone.

To that end, the term I've coined is the *inner guard*, because a guard can be both your protector and your jailor. You don't remember hiring the inner guard, but they are supposed to be here to protect you. There are times when you need protection, and with no inner guard, you'd have no conscience, no discretion, and no careful consideration of what might harm you. In this sense, there is no inner critic, only *inner criticism*. This is what the inner guard offers when they get scared and hypervigilant.

When the thoughts of doubt or negativity surface, what is the inner guard afraid of? How are they trying to protect you? I've come to learn that "assume positive intent" is not always a healthy position, because it can give a pass to toxic behavior and status imbalance. That said, there are times with trusted loved ones that seeking out the positive intent is still reparative. That's what I'm asking you to offer the inner guard. Especially with the harshest inner thoughts, the inner guard may be way off base and unhelpful; and yet, starting from a place of self-compassion may get you further than the combative stance of attacking an inner enemy. Remember the lesson of every Disney movie for the past decade: Your enemy is just a mirror of your own rage, looking to be understood.

IT'S NOT YOUR DEFAULT

What's going on in your brain to make the inner guard over-react? To move beyond semantics and metaphors, it helps to understand a bit about the brain's inner workings, especially for a creative mind. Your "Default Mode Network," or DMN, refers to the activity of an awake-but-resting brain. A mind that is not engaged in activity is seen to take a particular neural pathway or pattern. The energy expenditure between a resting brain and an active brain is not drastically different, unlike the difference between a brain in the waking state versus a brain in the sleeping state. The regions of brain activity, though, seem to show higher or lower activity depending on whether you are engaged in action. While the DMN has become a hot topic of debate in recent years, the research goes back to the 1970s, when Dr. David Ingvar first subjected participants to neuroimaging scans while at rest and while at work and traced their cerebral blood flow. While at rest, the activity in the frontal lobes (the area responsible for expressive language, executive functions, emotions, memory, and voluntary movement) increased. Hence daydreaming, memories, and grandiose or tragic visions of the future flood our brains when the DMN takes over. Just sit back and observe the narratives that effortlessly unfold with no specific stimuli to direct your attention.

People suffering from depression, for example, show increased levels of activity in their DMN. A schizophrenic DMN shows an overactivity of the brain where thought patterns are directed internally. Sometimes, these thoughts and sense perceptions get muddled up, leading to the hallucinatory experiences that come with this disorder. A brain that suffers from attention deficit hyperactivity disorder (ADHD), on the other hand, shows atypical connectivity in their DMN that affects the functions involved in attention and cognitive control.

The high-level cognitive areas that are activated in the DMN include the medial prefrontal cortex, posterior cingulate cortex, and parietal regions. The posterior cingulate cortex (PCC),[x] specifically, shows the most activation when subjects are prompted to think of their narrative, "autobiographical" self. Dysfunctions in the PCC are linked to major depression and anxiety, and some studies show a relationship between the self-criticism isolated in the dorsolateral prefrontal cortex and the PCC, so we can speculate that phantoms of imposter syndrome would feel right at home in the Default Mode Network.

I know, yikes, we're throwing around diagnoses I have no business delving into, and it may start to sound like the DMN stands for... Danger... Mind... Nope (sorry, I thought I had it). But in case you're thinking of a *Severance*-esque procedure to just annex the DMN and live in lobotomized bliss, we have to consider the sunny side of the DMN.

Since the narratives, recollection, daydreaming, and projection all take place within the DMN, this network is also the most active *during creative processes*. But to consume and make sense of imagination requires the work to have a certain structure and form. Hence with creativity, the DMN sets up a joint venture with the Executive Control Network in the brain. Both these complex networks work together to help turn your stream of consciousness and visions into language, music, movement, or mediated images.

Consider how this makes imposter syndrome especially potent for artists: Creativity requires you to tap into the DMN for new connections and novel expression, and yet that same DMN plays a significant role in rumination and negative thought spirals. As Joseph Campbell said, "The cave you fear to enter holds the treasure you seek." That dark cavern of the subconscious harbors your creative treasure, but if you linger there too long, the tide rises and the cave begins to flood.

It feels fitting, then, that the threshold of the imagination also stands as an arena for our battles with the inner guard. As we'll explore in coming chapters, ideally you can drop into creative flow, which seems to mute the guard for a spell; but at some point, you'll feel an urge to go a few rounds of shadow boxing with that inner voice. Finally, after you've built up a sweat, again make peace with your shadow. Maybe try *shadow hugging*.

Like a dream where every character is a version of yourself, the dark corners of the psyche also stage projections of our outward critics. As humans, we are built to refer to others for validation. When we are in a crowd and hear a loud bang, we first search for the expressions of the people around us. If we see a chainsaw-wielding clown, we run (*toward or away, depends on your predilections*). If we hear laughter, we are more confident in laughing out loud with them. Similarly, your inner guard latches on to validate the criticism of others, primed with a negativity bias that gives at least 3:1 odds for negativity over praise.[xi] Yes, feedback helps, but no one can tell you objectively how good, bad, or effective your work is. They can only tell you *how they respond to it*. Once you see a clear pattern of responses, however, you have a strong indication of what to change, what to cut back, and what to build on.

PUT IT INTO PRACTICE

Trying to sort out all the feedback you've received over the years? Download the **Creative Courage Feedback worksheet** at **accomplishedcreative.com**. In it, I'll walk you through what to consider, how to process it, and how to apply it to positive improvements in your self-image and work.

For a creative, this sense of unworthiness can become a slow-motion python, cinching and strangling inch-by-inch. I once met a talented photographer after an improv show. I'd seen his photos before, which were stunning, so I asked if photography was his primary profession. He furrowed his eyebrows and almost recoiled. "No, photography isn't my main gig!" he said. "Do you *improvise* for a living?" It seemed like his response was rooted more in defensiveness than in taking offense to what I said. When he asked if I improvised for a living, that was supposed to be a sharp retort, but his question made me reflect. I've been practicing improv since I was 16 (before that, my life was scripted), and I can honestly say that the skills I developed in storytelling, collaboration, creativity, and over-all confidence are what propelled me into radio, writing, and leadership development. So my answer is *yes*, I do improvise for a living. But what makes that notion of being a professional creative so repulsive for some?

An emerging artist follows two drives: self-expression and belonging. These two drives are drawn by their inevitable collision. To be a creative calls for an authentic representation of your inner worlds and perspectives, and to go beyond the shallows, these perspectives need to address an acute sense of suffering, redeemed at least in part through creativity. Even if your work shines, sparkles, dazzles, and uplifts, it feels empty if it never casts a shadow. As Brene Brown observes, "Vulnerability is the birthplace of innovation, creativity, and change." But in connecting your drive for self-expression with your drive for belonging, that vulnerability can feel like a chasm. How could you dare ask others to exchange value for what you feel you lack?

To make a living through your expressions and art, you need to be accepted by those who are willing to pay—or more romantically, to *sponsor, grant, or endow*, as if the currencies are as invisible as the inspiration, yet still bound to a familiar social contract. That's where the tension can set you back or propel you forward.

STOP FAKING IT AND START MAKING IT

> *Give me the confidence of a mediocre white man.*
> —Leigh Anne Jasheway

I would say this is particular to art, but it also holds true for management, marketing, and philosophy—any realm where our aspirations are invisible. Sometimes, it's hard to distinguish between brilliant insights met with wide acclaim, or *just getting away with it.*

Don't panic. No one is getting away. Blame it on conscientious inquiry, but eventually it will all circle back to this, to our questioning of the aesthetic social contract. Where my intent is exhausted and your comprehension is strained, there is a bridge. We agree to meet in the middle as long as truth or beauty or healing make the meeting worthwhile.

The bridge appears when the painter and the patron stand shoulder to shoulder in front of the canvas. What if, after the pique of inspiration has passed, the artist fears her work is just pretense? What if the patron doesn't "get it," but dreads confessing his ignorance? If this is a formal gallery, there's a long supply chain of inference between creation and display. In this example, we'd look to gallery owners, curators, critics, and collectors, among others, to each influence the value and perception of the work. If you're a musician, poet, sculptor, or acrobat, you can translate those roles for your industry: The "gatekeepers."

The dynamic tensions of producing art in the mainstream are centuries old. The tensions at the heart of the art and entertainment industries sway with both aesthetic standards and the supply and demand of attention. In decades past, that last sentence would have landed on "profit," but let's be honest, the most prevalent gatekeepers today are the algorithms. Social media trains us to jut our chins out for the flimsiest convictions, like, "The moon is a cancelled parade. Don't @ me." (I know that no one says "don't @ me" anymore, and when they did, it was like, *Ha ha, imagine if I brook no dissent for THIS, that I would die on this hill. RIP me. I'm dead*.) But there's something in that @, a spiral gate that no one can enter. We all want attention and we all have our guards up in case that attention comes.

So what signal can you offer to cut through the noise? We have American science fiction author Theodore Sturgeon to thank for "Sturgeon's Law," which tells us that "ninety-percent of everything is crud."[xii] Of the millions of thumbs swiping through the streams, how many of them will pause and catch on your call for attention?

Aha, so if you can master this "one weird trick" or the latest marketing ploy, you can blow right past your imposter syndrome and just sink into the dopamine bath of virtual attention? Or what if a genie—those magical beings famous for having no caveats to their blessings—suddenly granted you talent, wealth, and fame? Would that soothe your self-doubt? Well, let's test that. It's time for:

IMPOSTER SYNDROME: *Celebrity Edition*

Each of these descriptions and quotes come from interviews with famously talented and celebrated artists. Can you guess the origin of each quote in the style of *Unnamed Television Quiz Show?*™

> 1. This poet and author had the following to say about this condition: "I have written 11 books, but each time I think, 'Uh oh, they're going to find out now. I've run a game on everybody, and they're going to find me out."[7]

> 2. In 1972, at the height of his fame, this iconic and celestial rock star said, "Sometimes I don't feel as if I'm a person at all. I'm just a collection of other people's ideas."[8]

---

[7] Who is Maya Angelou?
[8] Who is David Bowie? (This honestly sounds like something your niece would say to make you feel old.)

3. This American tennis star had a hard time creating her identity as she felt that she fell under her elder sister's shadow. "It was tough for me to stop being [my sister] and become the person I am."[9]

4. Despite winning an Oscar and being one of the world's most beloved personalities, this actor said, "No matter what we've done, there comes a point where you think, 'How did I get here? When are they going to discover that I am, in fact, a fraud and take everything away from me?'"[10]

5. If someone shook you awake at 3 a.m. and asked you to name a famous scientist, you'd probably scream and tell them to get out (but still, this name would come to mind). Meanwhile, this legendary physicist once said, "The exaggerated esteem in which my lifework is held makes me very ill at ease. I feel compelled to think of myself as an involuntary swindler."[11]

While reading these quotes and matching them to the staggering talent behind them, how did you react? Were you dumbfounded, wondering how someone with that many accomplishments, millions of fans, and bobble-head figurines in their likeness could possibly doubt themselves? Right. The inner guard doesn't vanish with external validation—they just take on new forms and still find a way to undermine reality.

---

[9] Who is Serena Williams? (Yes, tennis is an art, and Serena is an artist.)

[10] Who is Tom Hanks? (You haven't been reading ahead with these footnotes, right?)

[11] Who is Albert Einstein? (Now kindly leave through the window.)

I BET THIS ROLLER COASTER ONLY GOES UP!

*Let the world close the doors you were not meant to walk
through, and walk through the ones that remain open.*
–Jay Shetty

In my own fumbling journey into semi-recognition, I started out at 18-years-old as a tour train conductor in Spokane's Riverfront Park. Every day, I'd tow gaggles of tourists around the clock tower, the historic Loof Carousel, and the old Expo Pavilion, all while cracking jokes that I assumed no one heard.

One day, during one of my routine train tour stops, a passenger approached and told me he was the program director for my favorite radio station, *105.7 The Peak*, which at the time cranked out my favorite '90s alt-rock hits (you know, Goo Goo Dolls, Foo Fighters, Sarah McLachlan etc.). As it turned out, Scott thought I had a good voice and personality for radio, and he wondered if I'd like to intern for the station.

While working through college, I ended up the overnight DJ for The Peak for almost four years. I also sometimes stayed past my overnight shift and produced the morning show, creating characters and bits for the hosts.

After college, I moved to Seattle with zero prospects, but after a series of temp jobs, my alt-rock DJ experience was enough for me to creep into public radio. I hosted "Weekend Edition" for KPLU ("NPR News and all that jazz") while still holding down an admin job at a hospital and working my way into the local improv and slam poetry scenes.

Then I decided I should be on *All Things Considered*. Okay, if that wasn't a record scratch that made you spill your NPR mug all over your NPR tote bag, I should explain that *All Things Considered* (ATC) is a national program with millions of listeners heard worldwide. My hubris at the time was like a little league pitcher deciding he suddenly wanted to be on *All Things Considered*. Still, somehow, it worked.

"We like this! Now, who are you?" That was essentially the reaction from ATC's commentary editor after I first blindly sent her my pitch from my Yahoo account. My first commentary (which you can still find online somewhere) was a satirical exploration of defaulting on my student loans and offering the government to repossess my education. As a 22-year-old white guy, I was undaunted by any doubt, any second-guessing that maybe I didn't have the experience, track record, or wisdom to warrant airtime on a global platform. I continued my momentum with a handful of commentaries and a couple of national stories, confusing my position as either a renegade opinionator or a strait-laced journalist. I also started winning poetry slams, performing weekly in improv shows, and eventually got the call to perform on HBO's *Def Poetry*. It was a blur, and rarely did I pause to wonder where it all was heading.

It turns out I didn't have to stop—or rather, it all stopped for me. A decade after my first national success, after years of a full-time public radio gig, sub-viral humor publications, and a musical I wrote for grad school, eventually it just... dried up. Maybe I pissed off one of the Muses or accidentally keyed her car, because I rarely had any inspiration. Oh, I did get married and collaborated on the successful debut of two amazing works of art named Julieta and Mariana, and for them I'm eternally grateful. Still, my identity as a creative now felt sporadic, or something I had and lost, like an aging boxer throwing feints at his shadow and somehow losing.

In the coming chapters, I will share what lifted me out of my creative drought. For now, I want to reflect on this specific stage in a creative career and why imposter syndrome seems most prevalent *after* we have ample evidence for our accomplishments. Most of my coaching clients and those I surveyed and studied for this book are mid- to late career, looking back on what they have created. They are either doubting the validity of past accomplishments, afraid they no longer have "it," or are tempering their self-appointed legacy with forced humility. If you are just starting out, there's room and insight for you here as well. I hope the research and reflections set the stage for your fruitful creative arc, possibly wondering if you have the momentum to emerge or second-guessing your inherent optimism.

That operative word, "emerge," plays many roles in the thrust of this book. No matter how accomplished, we are all emerging. Whether still in school, entwined with traditional academic guidance, just now tinkering after years of hesitation, or looking back after decades of service, if you take the briefest inward moment you will recognize the pattern of emergence.

At the most atomic level, neuroscience remains baffled with an absolute definition of consciousness, and yet *emergence* surfaces as a consistent foothold on an icy ascent. Todd Feinberg shares a brief synopsis of neurobiology's century-old shrug emoji:

> Despite some of life's unique features (Mayr, 2004) all basic life processes remain in principle explainable within the constraints of normal physics and chemistry. However, while the scientific basis of life is no longer a philosophical or scientific mystery, in the case of consciousness—more specifically in the case of subjective experience (phenomenal consciousness, primary consciousness, raw "feelings" or irreducible "qualia") – there appears to be what philosopher Levine (1983)

called an "explanatory gap" between the subjective experiences and the physical brain.[xiii]

Zooming out, we each emerge both from the world and into it, then emerge into our roles and expectations, then into our defiance or self-expression. Sometimes, emergence means stepping across a threshold. Sometimes we are pushed. For high performers, that ambiguity between self-propelled emergence and the whims of external forces places us in the crux of imposter syndrome.

A study conducted at Martin Luther University Halle-Wittenberg (MLU) by Personality and Individual Differences psychologists examined 76 participants who had self-diagnosed with imposter syndrome (though this is not a mental illness by any means). These participants were subjected to a range of intelligence tests, and the researchers rigged the results to always be positive, regardless of how participants had actually performed. When asked how they were able to perform so well, each of the subjects accredited their success to external phenomena such as luck instead of their own inherent attributes.[xiv]

As W.B. Yeats reminds us, "The best lack all conviction, while the worst/ Are full of passionate intensity." Or, as Charles Bukowski put it (for those who forgot about Yeats), "The problem with the world is that the intelligent people are full of doubts, while the stupid ones are full of confidence." This is what I call *the imposter paradox*: The fact that you are self-aware enough to doubt yourself suggests that you are more likely to be authentic. True frauds never waste a moment in doubt. How often do you see a con artist pause and ask, "Am I authentic and ethical? Am I doing the right thing?" I'm sure they have their dark and introspective moments, but for the most part they are *confidence artists*—they can only operate by smothering their conscience with a pillow and walking through the world convinced that they are worthier than their victims.

For the moment, I'll give you the benefit of the doubt that you are not a con artist and that your sense of self, ethical limits, and personality all fall within a "normative" range.[12] But, if you're still among the 70% who can't shake this self-inflicted feeling of fraudulence, then start by reframing. You can find ample resources on Cognitive Behavioral Therapy (CBT) theory to go deeper into reframing your narrative, ideally with the help of a therapist. But who needs to invest all that time and money when I could just give you a listicle? Start with these CBT themes to see if they inspire you to explore further:

- Understanding the motives that drive the behavioral patterns.
- Facing your deep-seated fears and questioning the underlying assumptions.
- Learning to identify the thoughts and the emotional responses that define the problem.
- Understanding the motivation of the behaviors of those who surround you.
- Learning and developing positive coping mechanisms.
- Documenting your strengths and developing stronger self-confidence.
- Quantifying your negative and positive emotions (e.g. on a scale of 1–10), checking them against common "thinking traps," and then reassessing the "score" of the emotion.

---

[12]   If you happen to be a psychopath, then no offense! Some of my best friends are psychopaths. No, wait. If you are my friend and think I'm talking about you, I'm definitely not. WHAT'S THAT OVER THERE? (*runs away from his own book*)

Organizational psychologist Adam Grant draws on the research of Carol Dwek and recommends countering imposter syndrome with a growth mindset: "A fixed mindset says, 'I don't know what I'm doing. It's only a matter of time until everyone finds out.' A growth mindset says, 'I don't know what I'm doing yet. It's only a matter of time until I figure it out.'" Later, Grant adds:

> Imposter syndrome isn't a disease. It's a normal response to internalizing impossibly high standards. Doubting yourself doesn't mean you're going to fail. It usually means you're facing a new challenge and you're going to learn. Feeling uncertainty is a precursor to growth.[xv]

If you never feel uncertain, you're complacent. If you're complacent, you're not growing, not creating, not connecting with others. If you're here to express and share meaning with the world, why are you wasting time chasing the ghost of perfect certainty?

MINIMUM VIABLE PRACTICE: WHAT'S THE POINT?

> *Mauve takes offense at my having said, 'I am an artist'—which I do not take back, because that word included, of course, the meaning: always seeking without absolutely finding. As far as I know, that word means: 'I am seeking, I am striving, I am with all my heart.'*
> –Vincent Van Gogh

What is your purpose? That is, why create at all? This is one of those questions that should make you shake your head and say, *That's a stupid question, Jeremy. Obviously, I create because...* *wait. Damn.*

OK, here's an experiment: Stop pursuing your art for a while. Take a break and starve your creativity. If that sounds unbearable, then you are driven by something perpetual, independent of judgment or reward. Can a flicker of self-doubt rob you of that drive? If you really are someone who can't live without your art, it will break out of you and you will find your canvas. You are your own gatekeeper. If that gate has rusted over, tangled with vines in the foreground of an abandoned estate, then now is the time to back up the truck, throw it back into drive, and FLOOR IT.

Do you see the contradictions in finding your purpose and tending to the masses as a sea of scarecrow critics? These contradictions do not mean that one set of values is true and the other is false. These contradictions simply highlight the conflicts that a successful creative needs to work through.

This is your minimum viable practice for overcoming imposter syndrome: Accept now that you will wade through resistance, doubt, regret, shame, and stretches of fallow inspiration, all the time knowing that the only way out is through. Remember why you started, and honor that origin every time you feel the urge to quit.

WHOA THERE! (OVERDOING IT)

Let's say you've already applied what you've learned here, your inner guard is suddenly your inner bestie, and you are flying high on unconditional confidence.

I CAN CONQUER ANYTHING!
EVEN MANIA!
BOW BEFORE MY NEW-FOUND COURAGE!

Tread carefully. If imposter syndrome sits on one end of the self-image spectrum, on the other end is the *Dunning-Kruger effect*. Not to be confused with Freddie's off-brand cousin, *Dunning-Kruger* creeps up when your DMN sparks the right insights, but your executive network is slacking and the artistic skill set just isn't there. Can you think of a celebrity or politician who runs entirely on ego and has no self-awareness? This is not a new phenomenon, but in 1999, the artistic community declared themselves collectively SHOOK when rappers David Dunning and Justin Kruger dropped a banger of an album called *Unskilled and Unaware of It*.

Wait, hold on (*holds up a finger while checking texts*). Oh, apologies. My research assistant is telling me that Dunning and Kruger are psychologists, not rappers, and it wasn't an album but a research paper. Regardless, the subtitle of their paper says it all: "How Difficulties in Recognizing One's Own Incompetence Lead to Inflated Self-Assessments." In the subjects they observed, lack of experience and/or low skill levels created this grandiose effect, in that *they didn't know what they didn't know.*[xvi]

Before you latch onto this new label and proclaim, *Oh, that's probably my issue! I'm such a Dunning-Kruger*, recall again that your humility, curiosity, and willingness to buy my book are signs of your inherent self-awareness. In Chapter 2 we'll explore more of the artist's role in balancing courage, skill, and inspiration, but for now just consider that a lack of skill is not the dominant issue for imposter syndrome. Philosopher Brian Johnson observes the revelation when we recognize a lack of skill or accomplishment: "You know that gap between who you are and who you know you could be? Well... that gap (and the creative tension we feel as we acknowledge it) is the very source of our creativity."

Recognizing that everyone has to start somewhere, take a deep breath, measure out that gap with determination, and take a running leap.

THE BALANCING ACT

> *The universe buries strange jewels deep within us all,*
> *and then stands back to see if we can find them.*
> –Elizabeth Gilbert, Big Magic

If you have been a victim of the *Dunning-Kruger* effect, no shame. The beauty of waking up from this cognitive bias is the revelation that we can never stop learning. As opposed to the myth of Sisyphus, who was doomed to enact the world's first real-life GIF as he rolled the same boulder up and down the hill for eternity, we can at least find traction in our cyclical experience and mark the progress we're making:

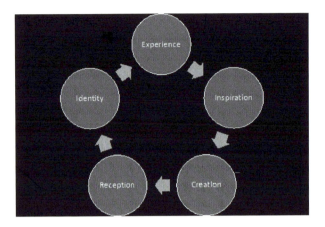

You experience your life, you find inspiration to frame and express your experience in an artistic way, you create, you distribute that creation (whether that's a blog post to the world or a poetry reading for your cat), others respond (commenting on your blog, licking themselves and walking away), and that feedback shapes how you refine your art or possibly even determines whether you keep creating. Importantly, you begin and end with *experience*, not an embalmed artifact. Once the piece is finished it is no longer yours to control.

You are not your art. Here you inherit the perpetual balance between making your work personal but not taking criticism too personally. At the same time, you can't simply say *forget the haters*, because eventually they'll resurface and you'll be caught in this *Eternal Sunshine of the Spotless Mind* loop with the haters, forgetting and remembering them in an endless, tortured cycle. Even when it stings, some critics have valid insights. The more you develop an authentic sense of self and a balance of ownership and distance from your art, the more you can respect when feedback resonates without internalizing it.

The writer Paul Valéry once said something to the effect that art is never finished, only abandoned. If that applies to your entire life as a creative, this abandonment is bleak. But as a cure for perfectionism, you can allow yourself only so long to remain tethered to the work, its reception, and its calls for revision. Or take a page from Jacques Derrida and release your work like you're releasing an animal into the wild. Perhaps *you* are the one abandoned, as your creation has another life to live without you. Otherwise, as you build up momentum your work starts to become your identity. You start to identify as an Artist, a Writer, a Sculptor, or a Dancer above all else (and yes, we can hear you capitalize the word as you say it), and your creativity gets wrapped up in your sense of self-worth—note that is your *sense* of self-worth, not your *actual* self-worth. This is where imposter syndrome is most likely to surface.

But just as you do for your art, you can employ your imagination to redraft your own origins. When an actor interprets a line, a pianist finds new depths in a chord, or a dancer takes a syncopated step, do you assume that's the way it's done and the way it will always be done? If not, then why does your rough draft of your self-image seem so static? The only true connection between who you are and what you create is that you are making it all up. So why not make this story a damn good one?

Remember to constantly shed your identifying tendencies. Its your ego's attempt at inflating itself.

I'm never an actor approaching a project or show, I'm a dude that likes to goof & get paid for it.

PUT IT INTO PRACTICE

Pick a project currently blocked by self-doubt. Then, using the **Accomplished Creative Workbook** at **accomplishedcreative.com**, gather evidence that you have everything you need to get started, learn or practice as needed, and astonish yourself again and again.

Chapter 2
The Unstoppable Artist— Inspiration and Influence

Leap and the net will appear.
–John Burroughs

There's a helluva universe next door. Let's go.
–E.E. Cummings

In his audio series *Clear Mind, Wild Heart*, poet and essayist David Whyte shares a conversation he once had with his mentor, David Steindl-Rast. They were up all night drinking wine, Whyte recalls, reflecting on the nature of literature and philosophy and mortality. At one point, Whyte turned to Steindl-Rast and said, "Speak to me of exhaustion." After a moment of reflection, Steindl-Rast said, "David, sometimes the answer to exhaustion is not rest. Sometimes the answer to exhaustion is *wholeheartedness*."

That line echoes every time I think I've exhausted my creative drive. Am I truly exhausted, or just half-hearted? Granted, my family also lives by the quote from Tom Parker: "If you don't know what you want, it's probably sleep." For now, though, let's suppose you're fully rested, caffeinated, buzzing from a good kettlebell workout, levitating off your meditation pillow, and filled with inspiration from this morning's reading, viewing, or visualization session. If you then approach the page, stage, or canvas and still feel deflated and seized with self-doubt, now what?

Here's what poet James Richardson might tell us:[xvii]

> When a jet flies low overhead, every glass in the cupboard sings. Feelings are like that: choral, not single; mixed, never pure. The sentimentalist may want to deny the sadness of boredom in his happiness, or the freedom that lightens even the worst loss. The moralist will resist his faint complicity. The sophisticate, dreading to be found naïve, will exclaim upon the traces of vanity or lust in any motive, as if they were the whole. Each is selling himself simplicity; each is weakened with his fear of weakness.

I like to imagine James dropping this truth bomb in a rap battle, the cipher circle falling out in disbelief, hands over mouths, doubling over, and *snap, snap, snap*, MC Richardson slays us all.

COURAGE, SKILL, AND INSPIRATION: CSI

To be *wholehearted* means finding a place for each of the heart's residents. Too often we're quick to evict boredom, vanity, or sadness because they aren't model tenants like inspiration, humility, and unconditional joy. But they each play a part. As long as you're not dwelling in the downswing, *resisting and persisting*, you'll find natural ways for the pendulum to swing back. Rather than flits of feeling, then, let's look at how your creative identity takes its cues from a triad of traits:

Courage, Skill, and Inspiration: You can call it *CSI* if you enjoy making witty, macabre quips before putting your sunglasses on in slow motion. These are the three traits of what I call The Unstoppable Artist. Then again, who calls themselves "stoppable?" *Wow, did you see that lackluster performance? I am stoppable today!* You know, we are all a bit stoppable now and then, but go with me on this and let's clear out what's stopping you:

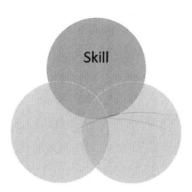

Skill without courage or inspiration: You might discover or develop a skill early on. Sometimes, this happens because you're drawn to a specific practice, or sometimes because a parent or teacher just handed you a paint brush or a clarinet and didn't give you a choice. This engenders the skill without confidence or inspiration, because you didn't choose this path and you don't have an inherent interest.

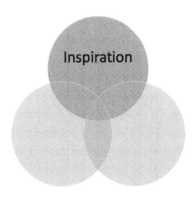

Inspiration without courage or skill: When you start with inspiration, you want to be creative and connect with others, and you may even know the subject matter and the tools and media you want to use. But if you don't yet have the courage to put this inspiration into practice or the skill to apply it, you're left adrift.

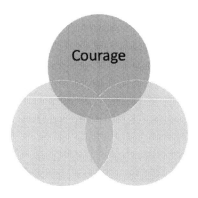

When courage dominates over skill and inspiration, you have an inner drive and a healthy sense of self; at least in your ability to conquer unseen dangers. We called my youngest daughter Danger Girl since she could crawl because she's always been fearless—climbing, exploring, giving her parents daily heart palpitations… you know the type. But maybe your courage came *before* the skill and inspiration because you didn't yet know how you wanted to channel all this energy.

> *A musician must make music, an artist must paint, a poet must write, if they are to be ultimately at peace with themselves. What you can be, you must be. This need we may call self-actualization. […] It refers to your desire for self-fulfillment, namely, to the tendency to become actually in what you are potentially: to become everything that you are capable of becoming.*
> –Dr. Edward Hoffman

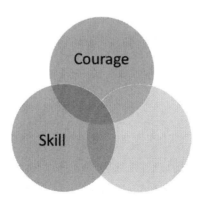

Courage and skill without inspiration: Here is where we start playing with propane and sparklers. Yet, as we approach the full unstoppable stack, this potential often creates our inner turmoil as artists, because it can be so subtle. What if you have the courage to create, you've proven you have the skill, but the inspiration just isn't there?

Some people object, *But Jeremy, if I have the courage, that means I'm inspired, right?* Not necessarily.

Courage is that global force, the rush, the drive, the risk-taking—and yes, it's related to inspiration—but inspiration for a specific creation is more personal; more intimate. When you are running on this energy from courage, and you know you have the skill to create but no inspiration, that can be especially difficult, because it feels like you're running in circles. You're burning energy, but not getting anywhere. It feels like you're jumping up and down in front of a blank canvas.

Let's say you do have the courage, you're running full steam, and you are inspired, certain of what you want to create and how you want to create it... But the skill level isn't quite there yet.

Notice I'm not talking about the *perception* of a skill gap. In this case, you can objectively see (and/or get trusted feedback) that you haven't had the training, the practice, the familiarity with other works of art in a specific discipline—and that is *fine*. You might just be passionate about a specific art or practice, and have no pretense about becoming professional or even highly skilled in that medium. (And, it's okay to be passionate about your art without making it a career!)

Like me with the piano, for example. Even with every piano app, method, live and virtual classes, and oh, right, *growing up with a mother who taught piano*, I just never got the hang of it. I tell people I'm like Linus on the piano. They say, "You mean Schroeder, the one who is always playing piano?" I say, "No, I mean Linus, the one with the blanket." It's unlikely I'll ever even want to perform for others, but I do enjoy playing. I just know the skill isn't there yet because I haven't given it the time and dedication. So if a true lack of skill is the issue, you have to embrace self-acceptance, patience, and humility to start somewhere.

Finally, we get to the core of imposter syndrome for most creatives. You have the skill and the inspiration, but you lack the courage.

I'm deliberate here when I say *courage* instead of *confidence*. Caroline Kennedy, founder and CEO of the organization Empowering Ambitious Women, explains it this way: "Confidence comes from believing we can do it; courage is giving it a go despite our fear."[xviii] While I'll show you several techniques for reframing your beliefs, we've already seen that perfectionists expect their beliefs to be unwavering. To cook up courage, fear is your first ingredient. Without fear, you wouldn't be courageous; only confident, or perhaps arrogant or bordering on *Dunning Kruger* territory.

THE IMPOSTER INVENTORY

> *Buddha nature, cleverly disguised as fear,*
> *kicks our ass into being receptive.*
> –Pema Chödrön

In my radio days, I once interviewed the mythology scholar Michael Meade, who shared one of the most powerful parables on fear and courage I've ever heard. When a lion becomes old and infirm, says Meade, they let the young pride move on while the elder waits alone in the tall grass. Then, when the elder sees prey, he quietly circles toward the far end of the younger lions until the prey stirs somewhere in between.

The elder lion roars. Knowing that the prey will run from the roar, the young pride waits for it to rush right into their ambush.

Each time, the prey falls victim to its own fear, not knowing that if it had run in the direction of the roar, it would have only faced an old, slow, and tired lion, rather than the young and ravenous predators awaiting it now.

According to Michael Meade, this common practice has long inspired local wisdom:[xix]

> 'Run towards the roar,' the old people used to tell the young ones. When faced with great danger and when people panic and seek a false sense of safety, run towards the roaring and go where you fear to go. For only in facing your fears can you find some safety and a way through. When the world rattles and the end seems near, go towards the roar.

Convinced? Let's run towards the roar. Since we've established that fear is the faithful companion to courage, we will face a few specific fears together to establish our Imposter Inventory.

For each of the following statements, rate how strongly you agree. Keep tabs of your answers on a sheet of paper, a notes app, or maybe hire a skywriter.

1. **I equate my identity with my creativity.**
   a. Strongly disagree
   b. Disagree
   c. Neither agree nor disagree
   d. Agree
   e. Strongly agree

2. **I need constant validation to create.**
   a. Strongly disagree

b. Disagree

c. Neither agree nor disagree

d. Agree

e. Strongly agree

3. **I often deflect praise.**

   a. Strongly disagree

   b. Disagree

   c. Neither agree nor disagree

   d. Agree

   e. Strongly agree

4. **I obsess over criticism.**

   a. Strongly disagree

   b. Disagree

   c. Neither agree nor disagree

   d. Agree

   e. Strongly agree

5. **I feel as if my "artist self" is different from who I truly am.**

   a. Strongly disagree

   b. Disagree

   c. Neither agree nor disagree

   d. Agree

   e. Strongly agree

6. **If people admire me for my art, I feel like a fraud.**

   a. Strongly disagree

   b. Disagree

   c. Neither agree nor disagree

   d. Agree

   e. Strongly agree

7. **In my art, I play it safe because I don't want to risk vulnerability.**
   a. Strongly disagree
   b. Disagree
   c. Neither agree nor disagree
   d. Agree
   e. Strongly agree

Now, add up your total.

- Each 'a' answer is worth one point
- Each 'b' answer is worth two points
- Each 'c' answer is worth three points
- Each 'd' answer is worth four points
- Each 'e' answer is worth five points.

Based on your total, here's what this survey can tell you:

Score	Results
7–10	All good
11–15	All good
16–20	All good
21–25	All good
26–30	All good
31–35	All good
36+	You did the math wrong, but all good!

One real takeaway: Most personality tests are bullshit, and many are biased toward non-Western cultures.[xx] Boxing yourself in with so-called "tests" may be a harmless conversation starter, but doing so also runs the risk of further constraining your sense of self by wrapping you in yet another label. "The ego likes little boxes it is familiar with," writes Stuart Wilde. "But when considering an infinite consciousness, the first thing you have to do is burn the boxes."

That said, the prompts I provided here are based on real surveys I took from artists dealing with imposter syndrome, although those were more qualitative and drawn from open-ended answers than the abbreviated quiz above. Let's take a beat to examine a few of these.

Equating your identity with your expression

In other words, you believe that if your art is good, then you're a good person, and if your art is lousy, then logically, you must be a terrible person. By extension, you believe that anything others say about your art, they are saying about you as a person.

Courage check: Even if your art is an expression of your deepest feelings and experiences, it's still only one limited, isolated, fragmented piece of your experience. Sometimes, that fragmentation blossoms into beauty. Regardless, your optimal self is infinitely larger than anything you create.

You need constant validation to create

You always need someone giving you praise, thumbs up and hearts on social media, or a parade down Main Street, or else you feel like there's no point in making or sharing your art.

Courage check: Positive encouragement is vital, but when your need for validation outweighs your service to the creation, then you start to drain a vital life force. The world owes validation to what is valid, meaning authentic. If you're too thirsty for praise, your authenticity wanes.

You deflect praise

Even if you do get that validation, your inner guard won't let you accept it. You assume others are just flattering you, or they don't understand the technical flaws that only you can see, and no amount of external praise will change your mind.

Courage check: I once shared this Bruce Lee quote with a tough English professor: "Forced humility is false pride." He looked at me dumbfounded: "You sound like you're quoting a fortune cookie!" We were both right. Deflecting praise doesn't make you humble; it makes the person offering sincere praise suddenly feel wrong or inferior.

You obsess over criticism

In a flurry of positive comments, you'll latch onto one negative remark and ruminate over it until it outweighs every nice thing that anyone ever said to you.

Courage check: Giving more weight to the negative over the positive is human nature. Harvard researcher Shawn Achor calls this the Losada line, named after psychologist Marcial Losada. In extensive testing, Losada and his associates studied reactions to feedback and determined that we need 2.9013 positive interactions for each negative interaction to maintain a positive outlook.[xxi] Let's round that up to three. You "need" at least three positive reviews for each negative one, but once you adjust for that cognitive bias, you can use tools like The Accomplished Creative Feedback Filter to determine what's relevant.

If people admire you for your art, you feel like a fraud

This is basically the *2018 Remix Featuring David Guetta* of forced humility. *Oh, you experienced my creative work and you like me? You must be gullible!*

Courage check: The crux of imposter syndrome hangs on that moralizing term "imposter," as if you are deliberately posing as someone to manipulate others. But this also presumes a staggering transcendence of the "Theory of Mind" phenomenon. In short, psychologists and philosophers would ask, *How do you know what others are thinking and feeling*? How do you know what characteristics or conditions they are perceiving to decide on their positive feelings toward you?" Try accepting their goodwill for a moment and assume it's authentic. Deeper still, this is tied into:

You feel as if your "artist self" is different from who you truly are

This is such a tempting trap, because any artist knows how it feels when they are in that zone of creation, that "flow" state of inspiration and courage and skill all converging... and you know, it comes and goes. Sometimes, you're elated and channeling pure inspiration, and you're delighted with the results. Your work is applauded, perhaps even profitable, and you can't help but ride that dopamine high.

Then later, after the big opening, the reading, or the concert, you're back home alone, the dopamine has flushed from your system and... you're just not feeling it. That down feeling is part of the cycle, but sometimes it lingers for a while, and you feel so separated from that person who was at their creative peak.

Courage check: That neurochemical cocktail of mood cycles may make you feel like an entirely different person. This happens because the "lauded artist" side of you is the one drawing in all of these positive associations, and you again fall for that "ideal self" trap in yet another disguise. But as you navigate these cycles and seasons, consider what your art would be without the *wholehearted you.* This is not to romanticize depression, addiction, or self-sabotaging behavior (again, these issues are best addressed with professional guidance), but rather to take the dips in mood and energy as a sign to be receptive, recovering, and accepting, and to give your inspiration some well-earned incubation.

You play it safe with your art to avoid vulnerability

Oof, I know. This one hits differently. That's because it calls out a real possibility: If you're not putting yourself out there, if you are hiding behind clichés or surface expression, then you might be an imposter.

Wait, did I just write that in the middle of a book about overcoming imposter syndrome? Yes, and I hope you'll trust me more for the candor, because I've read too many books on this topic that are wall-to-wall reassurance and unconditional cheerleading, bombarding you with insistence that *you're not an imposter, no one's an imposter, we are all authentic and pure and made of radiant light, rah rah rah*!

I will say that you are... *probably* not an imposter. That said, there may be moments or even stretches of time when we each pose or project in inauthentic ways, and in that snapshot of experience, perhaps the "imposter" label is the cold bucket of ice we need to shake us out of our complacency. You see how I slipped into the first-person plural, there? I am not absolving myself.

Going back to the posture metaphor from the introduction, if you are able-bodied and capable of "correct" posture, but you start to slouch from exhaustion, is that your new posture from now on? Likewise, the tendency to shrink away from your authentic voice or raw story is a product of fear that you can unlearn. Mary Karr, one of the most searing memoirists of our time, refers to the inauthentic posing of some writers as a retreat into obscurity—that is, obscure not in reputation, but obscure in their expression. "About real mystery," she writes in *The Art of Memoir*, "a writer can say every dang thing she knows without lessening the enigma's power; obscurity is just hiding out of cowardice what fundamentally needs unveiling."

Later in the book, Karr cites George Saunders from his 2013 MFA Graduation speech at Syracuse University:[xxii]

> We apply certain kinds of pressure to you, under which you are forced to flee to your highest ground. . . . But hopefully, under that pressure, you leave behind all of the false You's—the imitative You, the too-clever You, the Avoiding You—and settle into that (sometimes, at first, disappointing) beast, Real You. . . . Real You is all you have, and all other paths are false. And in the best case, Real You is so happy to finally be recognized, it rewards you with Originality.

As we've established, the "Real You" isn't so easy to spot in a lineup, nor is authenticity singular, but Saunders is onto something. The retreat is a reaction to pressure, to projected expectations, to the walls closing in so close that we can't separate our voice from the echoes.

To break free, we need to summon creativity to bust through those walls like the Kool Aid Man *(Ooooh, yeah)*. When the bricks and dust settle, we can squint into the sunlight and finally step into our journey.

BREATHE IT IN

It is difficult to get the news from poems, yet men die
miserably every day for lack of what is found there.
—William Carlos Williams

What speaks to you? Scratch that. *What sings to you?* It might be a work in your genre or something entirely unrelated. For me, while writing this book I was devouring stacks of brilliant works on psychology, philosophy, and creativity, and yet the one book that kept singing to me was *A Swim in a Pond in the Rain* by George Saunders. I could only get through two or three pages at a time without putting it down and writing a few paragraphs of my own—largely unrelated to the topics in Saunders' book, but still in tune with a shared energy. Why would close readings of Russian short stories be the key to my creative flow? I won't overthink it (famous last words). I just know that resonance isn't logical, and it takes a certain centeredness to find it for yourself.

But I am wholly original, you insist. *Leaning too much on inspiration will make me derivative!* That's one line of thought, and it's another sign that your inner guard has sharpened their ventriloquism skills. After all, even a nod to influence means you might start comparing yourself to The Greats. In his 1973 work *The Anxiety of Influence*, the infamous Yale professor and author Harold Bloom[13] insisted that nearly all modern literature was a "misreading" of Shakespeare, Milton, and a handful of others deemed worthy of Bloom's Western Canon.[xxiii] Three decades later, Jonathan Lethem countered Bloom with an essay called *The Ecstasy of Influence*, arguing that echoes, repurposing,

---

[13] I spent about a year writing a play about Harold Bloom and Jacques Derrida, laced with cultural studies and anti-racism. It was described as "smart and funny and hard to follow." Nailed it!

remixing, and reimagining are all inherent to creation, and that we should embrace our influences as we add to the narrative.[xxiv] I won't quote directly from Lethem's essay for reasons that are tough to explain until you've read the entire thing. However, I encourage you to search it out on *Harper's* and tell me you're not startled and inspired.

The word *inspiration* derives from the Old French word *inspiracion*, "inhaling, breathing in; inspiration," and from the Latin *inspirare*, "blow into, breathe upon." With every breath, inspiration flows through both the huffing and the puffing. (Let's keep this in mind when we explore meditation in Chapter 4.) This also merges with the influence debate when we consider the staggering physics and history of oxygen. In *Caesar's Last Breath*, author Sam Kean calculates the diffusion of Julius Caesar's dying gasp in 44 BCE, the path and transformations those molecules would make (about 25 sextillion), the properties of circulation and atmosphere over centuries, and a dazzling series of computations and analogies to make this case: "When you crunch the numbers, you'll find that roughly one particle of 'Caesar air' will appear in your next breath."

Wait, what? I know. It's bonkers. But I did the math. Okay, I didn't do the math, but I trust that Kean's fact-checkers and publishers did the math to keep the book in the non-fiction section, and it's just one of those baffling parlor tricks of science that jostles our preconceptions. Of course, it's not just Caesar, as Kean is using this one historical figure for dramatic effect. If we extrapolate, then, you and I are always giving and taking inspiration from billions of others we'll never meet. Can you avoid inspiration and influence? Don't hold your breath.

Still, we'll always have contrarians. Chuck Close, the American photorealist painter, once claimed that inspiration is for amateurs. What he meant was that artists shouldn't sit around and wait for inspiration, but instead forge the discipline of daily practice, putting in the reps whether you feel like it or not. I'm not sure who convinced Close that inspiration and discipline are mutually exclusive, but we could all benefit from practices that turn the daily grind into a creative spark.

MINIMUM VIABLE PRACTICE: THE MORNING PAGES

Let's say you stumbled across grainy security cam footage from a North Spokane Denny's restaurant in 1997: On any given Monday or Wednesday around 11 p.m., you'd see me sitting in a crowded booth, surrounded by my friends from Gonzaga University Theatresports. While everyone else laughs and tells stories, there's me with my gravy-covered hash browns and hot chocolate, hunched over the end of the booth, fiercely scribbling away in a spiral notebook. Such was my obsession with the Morning Pages.

Perhaps you've heard of the Morning Pages, or you even practiced them without knowing where they originated. Well, technically the idea of writing your stream of consciousness originated with the invention of the written word, but American author and poet Julia Cameron popularized this simple ritual as a deliberate invocation in her 1992 masterpiece *The Artist's Way*. Cameron refers to this practice as "the bedrock of creative recovery:"

> Morning Pages are three pages of longhand, stream of consciousness writing, done first thing in the morning. *There is no wrong way to do Morning Pages*–they are not high art. They are not even "writing." They are about anything and

everything that crosses your mind–and they are for your eyes only. Morning Pages provoke, clarify, comfort, cajole, prioritize and synchronize the day at hand. Do not over-think Morning Pages: just put three pages of anything on the page... and then do three more pages tomorrow.[xxv]

As you may have noticed from my Denny's tableau, I don't always finish my Morning Pages in the morning; that's a preference, not a mandate. In my first few years of following *The Artist's Way*, which includes dozens of practices, I was a Morning Pages zealot. I think my creative life improved as a result, if not my social life. Then, over the years, I fell out of practice at times before jumping back in with the fervor of the newly sober, until finally settling on writing my Morning Pages a few days a week.

Paraphrasing Joseph Campbell, artistic expression invites you to pry open your internal worlds and project them outward. Hence, the task of the artist is complex, intricate, and almost delicate. For any work crafted for an audience, it's easy to stop, reconsider, rehearse a few imagined criticisms, then erase all progress, trash the manuscript, burn down the studio, fake your own death, and escape to a new life on a Caribbean beach.

The Morning Pages offer nowhere to run. To that end, I'll simply add my own testimonial to Cameron's simple practice and gently suggest you start your own Morning Pages as your Minimum Viable Practice for inviting inspiration. Start tomorrow, and if you stop, forgive yourself and keep on starting.

OVERDOING IT: INSPIRATION AS CLICHÉ

If you linger in the throes of inspiration too long, you may succumb to the overwhelm of everything that's ever been done in your art form, the endless comparisons, and the oscillation between obscurity (as Karr warned us) and cliché. In my desultory modes between poet and critic, I've often said that clichés are victimless plagiarism. Ah, but really now, *victimless*? Anonymous, maybe. Obtuse, thudding, roundly bruised, pilfered, yawned, and regurgitated, perhaps, but hardly victimless. Distinction: The originator of the phrase or device (which was once innovative) and the reader of the threadbare attempt. Victims, both! What "victimless plagiarism" was, all along, was that cute effect of sacrificing caveats for aphoristic sting. It sounds good, sort of rolls along and pounces. Nevertheless, the sticking point for clichés remains a question of invention or theft. Moreover, with that moralistic term of "theft," like "imposter syndrome," I raise a more central question: When do aesthetics, in its appraisal of beauty, turn judgment toward the accountability of the individual? Do we believe Wittgenstein, that "ethics and aesthetics are one?" To limit my scope, I will attend here primarily to the question of innovation in artwork, how innovation is determined, whether it remains important, and indeed, what distinguishes innovation from originality. Is pure originality still possible in an Age of Influence? No surprises here: I contend that innovation, though not always wholly original, is still possible, and our task must be to ferret out the characteristics and criteria of innovation, recognizing that it is something more than caprice and something less than pure invention.

Innovation is relative, but it is not subjective. Relativity is a matter of comparison, recognizing what has come before or what stands parallel, tandem, designated for measure, or setting a criterion by example, be it good or bad. Subjectivity, rather, is that judgment which comes from the subject, a resonance coiled within a personal history, mostly unconscious, the "taste" of the individual. But what has been accomplished before is not a matter of taste. It is empirical. When critiquing an artistic move as "done before," I can say with conviction that Shakespeare or Milton or Morrison or Rich already coined a specific phrase, for example. Here we have records, empirical standards as text. There is nothing subjective about it. What a cliché accomplishes, in the crassest violation of originality, is the graft of a taxed phrase onto the canvas with a single, lazy gesture. An archetypal shrug. The subject as an artist may have an "original" intention behind the mimeographed phrase, but in aesthetics as in ethics, intention does not forgive effect. If you are drowning and someone intends to save you, but in ignorance throws a lunchbox instead of a life preserver, do you bless this fool for his intent to save, or do you recognize the emptiness of sentiment as you drown?

Clearly, we must demand more than intent. As Oscar Wilde said, "All bad poetry springs from genuine feelings." Oh, Harold Bloom relished that Wilde quote. The "genuine feelings" argument is the best summary in that gap between attempt and achievement, and more to the point, the defensive mechanism built into personal art. "But it means something to me," pleads the untrained poet. "But it's a true story," says the struggling novelist. Still. Regardless of the feelings behind them, these are not examples of originality. In isolating these subjective intentions, we can also see that the artist's familiarity with these expressions as unskilled or worn out is not a factor in our judgment of originality, though it may, in retrospect, offer them reprieve or erstwhile excuse.

Once artists recognize the established techniques and trends, the converse of cliché may be caprice or obscurity. In forceful rejection of tradition, an artist may attempt to shun all convention, give up on craft, rely instead on an intuitive reservoir of insight and find means of expression beyond all boundaries and expectation. But this untethered approach has its limits, as philosopher Roger Scruton observes:

> Originality is not an attempt to capture attention come what may, or to shock or disturb in order shut out competition from the world. The most original works of art may be genial applications of a well-known vocabulary ... What makes them original is not their defiance of the past or their rude assault on settled expectations, but the element of surprise with which they invest the forms and repertoire of a tradition. Without tradition, originality cannot exist: for it is only against a tradition that it becomes perceivable.[xxvi]

In his defense of tradition, Scruton speaks germanely to the role of context. From here, I'm going to take Scruton's ball and run with it, even if I'm running into a field he never intended his argument to play in. I want to acknowledge my cultural studies grad school friends who say, "Yes, and fuck tradition—and fuck the Western canon, the patriarchal constructs, and the Gramscian hegemony of it all." But without acknowledging our troubled antecedents, all that fucking is just thrusting our out-of-context pelvises into thin air. In short, how do you know you're original? How do you know what you're echoing, rejecting, or deconstructing? You step back, and you catch yourself before your heel catches over the edge.

THE BALANCING ACT: STEPPING OUT OF THE CROWD

All of this hand wringing about clichés is not meant to intimidate or admonish. To fall back on the familiar is a product of fear, of that displaced sense of belonging, trying to fit in by giving in.

Don't give in.

If your art is cliché, then you are answering that call for belonging by blending into the crowd, donning a beige cap and lowering your head to avoid detection. You're afraid of true self-expression because rejection starts with distinction. If they can't pick you out in the crowd, how can they banish you?

"Every breath is a prayer," say the mystics, and even the most secular among us can borrow this melody for our own lyrics: *Every breath is a door, an answer, a calling, a rift, an orphan clinging to a passing satellite*—whatever keeps you vigilant. This may be what Pete Holmes calls "nostalgia for the present." The courage to create, like balance, demands constant awareness (more global and flowing than strict attention), only with practice building more and more momentum until flow feels natural. As we break down the illusions of imposter syndrome, recognize the muscle we're developing in creative practice, and invite inspiration with every breath, we're left again with the blank page, empty stage, or pristine canvas.

But this time, we have an unfair advantage—the tools of limitless creativity.

Chapter 3
Building the Plane in Mid-Air— How to Think Like an Improviser

*According to the largest metanalysis of creativity ever done ...
[to enhance creativity] we need to be training a **state of mind**.*
–Steven Kotler

*If you wish to make an apple pie from scratch,
first you must create the universe.*
–Carl Sagan

For over 17 years, I performed two or three times per month in Theatresports, a weekly improvised show in Seattle's Pike Place Market. At that time the show ran from 10:30 p.m. to midnight, so there was always this raucous, late-night energy among the performers and the crowd. One night, I was warming up backstage before Theatresports and responded to an especially funny line with the lame retort, "Hey, save it for the stage."

Suddenly, our artistic director Randy Dixon turned and looked at me. "What do you mean, 'Save it for the stage?'" he responded. "Creativity isn't a bank—it's a muscle."

Like many insights or twist endings, Randy's insight was unexpected and inevitable. Of course creativity is a muscle! Yet it's so tempting to treat creativity as a bank we can rob or deplete, or as a reservoir subject to rations and drought. Here we are, each of us, walking around like delicate vessels who must save every drop of inspiration, terrified of spilling over or bursting forth, certain that if we do then it will never rain again.

In Chapter 7 we'll consider how our literal muscles and expressions of embodiment feed into our creativity. Right now, I want to stretch out the metaphor of muscle and how we can build, stretch, and mobilize our creative force.

- *Creativity is power.* The more you practice your creativity, the more powerful it becomes. As a construct of physics, you measure power by how much energy you transfer or convert within a unit of time.
- *Creativity is speed.* In this, I do not mean that creativity is rushed. I'm talking about the speed of connection, the speed of insight and innovation, the instantaneous, always-present power of creativity that you don't force, but rather discover and unleash.
- *Creativity is slow and controlled.* Again, creativity might embody speed, but it does not always happen quickly. Just like building muscle and mobility, sometimes you need to focus on slow and controlled movement—especially as you are refining your craft.
- *Creativity is balance.* This is a central mental model in forging our creative courage. As we touch on the balancing act in each chapter, we repeat again that we're not arriving at balance as a static place, but always moving toward or away from balance. Not "balance" as an inert noun, but to balance as perpetual energy.

WORKING IT OUT

Improvisational theater is the CrossFit of creativity, in that anyone who takes it up cannot shut up about it. It's also addictive, communal, and charged with endless variety. Many will tell you that improv saved their lives. Believe them. I mean, don't take their flyer, but believe them.

Beyond the popularized depictions in short-form comedy, over the past two decades I've taught applied improvisation to countless professionals in business, medicine, law, and mental health—any practice that can benefit from an infusion of innovation and embodied practice. Among my fellow ensemble members at Unexpected Productions in Seattle, most of them have careers outside of the arts.

One of my fellow ensemble members is Dr. Belinda Fu, a family physician, educator, and improv actor in Seattle. Belinda founded the organization ImprovDoc to teach improvisation skills to fellow clinicians. She's seen how the surprising insights from this practice can improve communication, cognition, and wellness for both the physicians and their patients. Most importantly, Belinda shares how improv transformed her life:

> When I finished my residency training, I started taking improv classes just for fun–little did I know that it would transform my life in wonderful ways. The skills I learned in improv made me a better doctor, teacher, and all around person. A few years later, when I became a patient with early-stage vulvar cancer, my life spun into turmoil, but the affirmation skills I learned in improv saved my life. Since then, improv skills have helped me

survive other challenging times, and to move my life forward in creative and healthy ways.[xxvii]

In a recent interview, Belinda also explained to me that improv taught her how to fail gracefully. In medicine, perfectionism runs rampant, because any mistake could have dire consequences, and because allopathic medicine has historically perpetuated a culture of personal shame around mistakes. ii The irony is that this mindset often provokes negative effects on health, performance, and wellbeing, potentially leading to burnout and depression. "We unintentionally practice becoming ashamed of ourselves or hiding our feelings like an imposter," she says. "And in improv, the antidote is to practice failing and regarding that as growth and opportunity and development, and constantly saying, 'Come as you are.'"

In recent decades, classes in applied improv have cropped up at multiple Master of Business Administration (MBA) programs, including Harvard Business School and the Wharton School of Business. A 2021 research study from business professors Pier Vittorio Mannucci, Davide C. Orazi, and Kristine de Valck identified three levels of improvisation skills applicable to organizational development:[xxviii]

1. **Imitative:** Usually the dominant mode for beginning improvisers, *imitative* refers to simple observation and replication of more experienced players without adding or expanding.
2. **Reactive:** Beyond imitation, reactive improvisation requires original, spontaneous responses to the environment or other players.
3. **Generative:** "Generative improvisation is about probing into the future and proactively trying new things

in an attempt to anticipate and even catalyze (rather than react to) what could happen," observe the authors. They see this as the highest of the three levels, carrying the most risk and offering the biggest rewards for innovation.

When I teach applied improv to business professionals, I often witness the typical reservations and eye-rolling from a few, but eventually they warm up to the group dynamics and lean into the energy of collaboration and creation that improvisation promotes. Formal course assessments usually highlight the benefits of the workshop for team building, presentation skills, problem solving, mindfulness, and overall confidence. A few come back for regular classes—improv has a way of getting its hooks into you.

THE IMPROVISING IMPOSTER

> *I can never be all the people I want and live all the lives I want.*
> *I can never train myself in all the skills I want. And why do I*
> *want? I want to live and feel all the shades, tones and variations*
> *of mental and physical experience possible in my life.*
> —Matt Haig, *The Midnight Library*

I first discovered improv while still at the halfway house, wedged inside our tiny room and marveling at the marathons of *Whose Line is it Anyway?* on our stolen cable; 11 years later I would perform on stage with *Whose Line* star Ryan Stiles, but at this point, I couldn't imagine myself taking those risks. I was astonished that anyone could create endless stories, jokes, and songs based entirely on random suggestions and a grab box of theater games.

In your first Improv 101 class, the instructor might share that old chestnut that "we're all improvising all of the time." That's true, and yet it wasn't until I stepped on stage for the first time that I first began to embody the self-actualization required to start making shit up in a structured way. I was 16, still getting into personal development and philosophy, and learning enough to be that arrogant faux-punk kid who quotes Bad Religion lyrics like a manic preacher.

Improv humbled me the way lightning humbles a sapling. The lessons were instant and the practice (so far) lasts a lifetime. Even if you never perform improv, the principles of the practice should resonate with anyone who creates on demand.

One of the first frameworks I learned was CROW, an acronym for considerations that carry beyond the stage:

- **Character**: Who are you in this scene? How are you showing up? How do your mannerisms, language, backstory, profession, and needs inform this moment?
- **Relationship**: Even if you're giving a monologue in a desert, at some point you'll need to consider relationships. More likely, you're sharing the stage. How do you define the relationship? Are you colleagues, sisters, arch nemeses, doctor and patient? Beneath that surface, what is your relationship status at this moment?
- **Objective:** What do you want? Can someone else in the scene provide what you want? How does that propel your choices in this moment?
- **Where:** Within the border of this stage, where are you? In a Denny's? A skate park? The moon? How does your environment inform your choices in this moment?

Before, after, and within each of these choices, you also follow the core philosophy of improvisation: *Yes, and*. For each offer or accident, you embrace it and add to it. Each volley, gesture, revelation, and leap into the unknown only spins up into a story when each participant is affirming and building. The most honest and grounded reactions set off a chain of chemical reactions and cascading dominoes of a narrative. What seem like simple asides become startling confessions. *Yes, and* builds an empire one affirmation at a time.

Uncertain about who you are and where you belong? Try stepping into a new identity dozens, hundreds, thousands of times. Go *Quantum Leap* with it. The most experienced actors will tell you that the art is more inward then outward, uncovering the parts of you that serve this character, this arc, this feeling processed through text and movement.

Rick Steadman, former Education Director for ComedySportz Los Angeles, recently shared with me how improvisation has informed his emotional growth. Rick is also a close friend going back 27 years, and I've been astounded by the trajectory of his career. In addition to the countless lives he's impacted as an educator, Rick has appeared in several national television series, including *Criminal Minds* and *Marvel's Agent Carter*. (Yes, he's technically part of the freaking MCU!) Still, he admits he can't shake that feeling of "never being good enough."

In an interview for my podcast, *Think Like an Improviser*, Rick reminded me of a conversation we had eight or nine years ago:

> I was talking about this feeling that I'd had, you know, for as long as I could remember... and you said, 'Yeah, imposter syndrome.' And I remember I burst out crying and said, 'It has a name?' Because it was that experience of like this kind

of deep, dark, ugly pain that I had been carrying around and rarely verbalizing... And then to like, to let it out into the sunlight and then be told, Oh yeah, not only is that a thing that other people experience, like there's a name for it... it deeply resonated with me.

For Rick, the tilt-a-whirl career of a Hollywood actor offers an unpredictable series of wins and losses. Each new role is exhilarating, and each "not a good fit" can feel like a deeply personal rejection. So if acting exacerbated his imposter syndrome, how could his creative pursuit also help rebuild his confidence?

With improv, Rick says, there's no time or headspace to be self-conscious. "When I am focused on the people that I am performing with, when I'm really focused on what they are doing and on listening to them and being affected by them and trying to communicate with them, when all of that is happening, there's no space for me [to overthink]." Rick adds that the improviser's credo is to "make the other person look good," so each person on stage is focused outward and supporting each other. On balance, they all look good by virtue of what serves the relationship, the scene, and the story. When Rick or any improviser masters that allocentric instinct, it informs how they see themselves and the world—not as the center of attention or rejection, but as a vital element of a larger creation.

YOUR BRAIN ON IMPROV

> *You're never more than one thought away from a*
> *completely new experience of being alive.*
> —Sid Banks

In 2008, Johns Hopkins University studied jazz musicians and freestyle rappers under functional magnetic resonance imaging (fMRI) and watched what happened when they switched from prewritten music to fully improvised music.[xxix]

Here's what happened when the musicians and rappers flipped into improv:

Were you thinking it's all about the dorsolateral prefrontal cortex? Yeah, I know, that's what we all assumed. Still, it's fascinating to consider how this flight into uncertainty opens these gates in the mind:

- **Lowering self-censoring:** Second-guessing doesn't get a vote here. Instinct is in the driver's seat and you are in *Fast and the Furious* nitro mode.
- **Muting inner criticism:** Fully engaged improv is like giving the inner guard a weighted blanket and a pacifier.
- **Reducing inhibition:** Courage becomes second nature. With the guardrails of instinctive skill and adaptation, you might even appear reckless at times, only to skid to a stop at the cliff's edge and pump your fist in victory.

Meanwhile, your brain is juicing up the following:

Your Brain on Improv

INCREASED ACTIVITY
Medial prefrontal cortex:
Self-expression
Self-narrative
Inner motivation

Ahhh, yeah, it's time for the medial prefrontal cortex to take the stage:

- **Boosting self-expression:** The core, creative, courageous parts of you, once huddled in the crawl space of insecurity, suddenly kick open the door and find that they're tandem skydiving over the bluest ocean.
- **Foregrounding self-narrative:** Even if the music, dance, or scene is not about you, great improv infuses the expression with a new chapter in your latest story.
- **Increasing inner motivation:** No longer waiting on external conditions, you blast open the gates and follow the dopamine drive through the leaps and loops of rewarded novelty.

Granted, memorizing neurobiology and the corresponding inhibitors and stimulators of creativity will not make you the most present improviser. As Charlie Parker said, "Master your instrument, then forget all that shit and play." Theory is one thing, but what we're really after is the unconscious competence, the groove, the pocket, the transcendent whir of selfless creation that just takes over and does its thing. What we're really after is *flow*.

GETTING INTO FLOW

Sorry, I forgot to warn you. Saying "flow" in the context of creativity causes a thousand bells to ring and confetti and balloons to drop from the ceiling (we rigged that the moment you purchased this book).

Flow is a term that psychologist Mihály Csíkszentmihályi coined in 1975 to describe a state of hyper focus and optimal performance.[xxx] Csíkszentmihályi defined flow as "the optimal state of consciousness where we feel our best and perform our best." In the decades since, psychologists, coaches, journalists, neuroscientists, philosophers, and personal development writers have explored methods for conjuring flow in sports, creativity, and the promotion of general well-being. While there is no surefire "switch" to bring you into that zone—and infatuation with optimal performance can leave you in the same defeated state as the perfectionist—there are a handful of flow characteristics that Csíkszentmihályi first suggested, with later additions from psychologist Keith Sawyer and author Steven Kotler.[xxxi] These flow triggers include setting clear goals, concentrating in the moment, identifying high consequences, and (in the case of group flow) constant communication and a shared sense or risk.

One characteristic of flow presents as especially relevant for artists who are grappling with creativity as a reflection of self-worth: The challenge/skills ratio. Let's look at a chart, shall we?

Pressure, Performance, and Flow

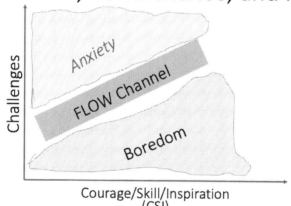

This chart, rendered even more authentic by my janky drawing skills, illustrates the scenarios that can limit creativity and exacerbate imposter syndrome due to an imbalanced challenge/skills ratio.

First, consider the challenges you're facing in a given work, event, or performance. The higher up on the Y axis, the harder the technical feat, the more risk, the more uncertainty—any factor that would make it more challenging.

Then we return to Courage, Skill, and Inspiration. Along the X axis, all three qualities come into play.

Researchers tell us that we can divide this into three sections. First, we have everything above the top line in the amorphous blob of my PowerPoint handwriting. You can see that represents high-to-extreme challenge combined with low-to-moderate skill, which tends to cause anxiety.

There are no exact measurements in this illustration, so obviously this is more conceptual, but it is based on real research.

Then you have everything beneath the lower line. In this area, we find low-to-moderate challenge and low-to-high courage, skill, and inspiration. That leaves you in the zone of boredom.

As you might anticipate, we've got our sweet spot between these two lines—not so challenging that it outpaces your skill, and not so easy that it leaves you uninspired. This is the Flow Channel, the perfect balance of challenge intersecting with your courage, skill, and inspiration. This is what helps your brain click into that perfect, focused, creative flow we are all searching for. If you recall the fickle nature of the Default Mode Network, its interface with executive control, and the art of that neurobiological ratio, then flow brings the DMN back into balance, away from rumination, and in service of our creativity.

"If you want to trigger flow," says Steven Kotler, "the challenge should be 4 percent greater than the skills."[xxxii] Why "4 percent?" You can follow Kotler's research in the citations to go down that rabbit hole, but for our purposes, it's an inspiring, accessible number to put you in the right mindset: Push your skills to the edge, then go just a bit further. At some point, you'll have to trust your instincts to recognize when you're in the zone.

All of the fascinating science aside, sometimes flow feels like yet another word for that fickle nature of creativity—fun to rhapsodize about but easily killed by overthinking it. The Zen scholar Sunryu Suzuki said, "Enlightenment is an accident, but some activities make us more accident prone." For Suzuki, those activities were focused on mindfulness (which we'll focus on in the next chapter). For improvisation, those activities that prime us for accidental enlightenment are theater games.

Bringing the theory back to practice, then, would you like to play a game?

WHAT ARE YOU DOING?

When I teach improvisation to non-improvisers—say, architects, doctors, lawyers, or software engineers—one of my favorite games to introduce is called "What are You Doing?"

Two improvisers step onto the stage and Improviser A asks for a suggestion for any solo activity. Let's say someone in the audience yells out, "Jumping rope!" The improviser then mimes jumping rope, and after a few seconds Improviser B asks, "What are you doing?"

According to the rules of this game, the improviser performing the activity cannot say the activity they are doing now, nor any activity they've already chosen during this round. The improviser has to say something "random." (I'll get into why I put "random" in quotes there in a moment, but let's play this out for illustration.)

When asked, "What are you doing?" the jump-roping improviser might respond, "Bird watching." Then, Improviser B starts holding up imaginary binoculars, referencing their bird watching book, squinting at the trees, etc.

But the moment Improviser A says, "What are you doing?" Improviser B has to scramble for a new activity, then prompt the other improviser, then take another activity and think of another novel suggestion that contradicts the description of their movements, until at some point the strain of reaching and forcing new ideas leads to the dreaded BLANKING OUT. When either improviser hesitates for more than a half-second, they are out of the game.

Let's zoom into the brain of Improviser B and consider their dilemma. Rather than "random," the next activity will stem from a specific association tactic. We'll call the first option "satellite thoughts:"

With "bird watching" front of mind, notice that each of the associations are satellites orbiting around the central thought. They are limited to a tight cluster of topics. Often, this is what I observe with beginning improvisers, and it leaves them with a limited runway for creative ideas.

As you're recognizing now, this game, "What are you doing?" is illustrating a phenomenon in the brain that happens in all sorts of idea-generation. That can be brainstorming, writing music, poetry, even abstract art—all these activities are about *association*, or the way we connect one idea to the next.

Let me give you a moment to try this game. When you get a chance, I recommend trying it with a friend or family member—or you know, with your cat, if no one else is willing to play along.

Let's say your suggestion is... "washing your car." Take a moment to imagine yourself miming this activity and really focus. Maybe close your eyes for a few seconds and then:

"What are you doing?"

See? You barely had a chance to think past your first thoughts, right?

The reason is that you had this suggestion, this anchor activity of washing a car, and maybe you pictured washing a car, and then thought of a sponge, a hose, soap, a driveway, the first or last time you saw someone washing a car...

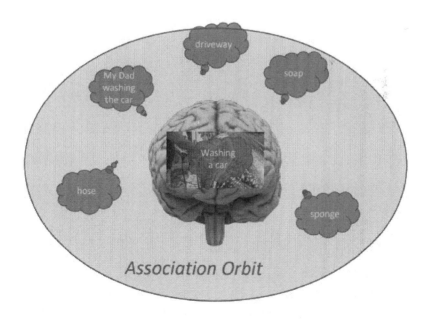

Association Orbit

This is all natural, but if you never travel out of this, you get caught in the *association orbit*. For some scenarios, like naming a product or stacking challenges that a character is facing, an association orbit may be fine. But if you've ever found yourself in a creative rut, especially a creative rut that you attach to your self-worth, being stuck in this one mode may be one of the unconscious factors holding you back and slowing you down.

Each time you generate a new association in "orbit" mode, you are reinforcing a circular thought pattern, also prevalent in negative thinking and rumination. As you'll recall, creative improvisation wants you to break free of that rumination and explore all possibilities.

On the other end of the extreme, then, you can experiment with the *association stretch*:

Association Stretch

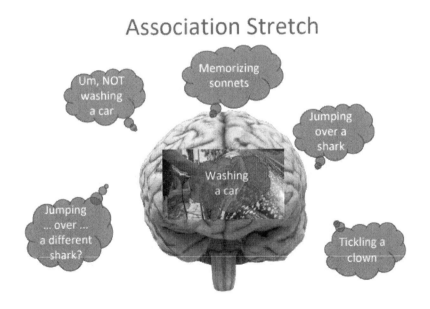

With a string of seeming non-sequiturs (though there must be some pattern of association your brain is churning out), you are stretching your imagination to come up with the most random ideas you can muster. This can be amusing and generative to a degree, but you can also recognize how it's a bit forced.

Now that I've shared two approaches that don't work, those of you playing the home version of the Personal Development Tropes are probably bracing for door number three, which will feature my breakthrough new approach, complete with a trademarked term and a merch store.

So let's get into it.

ASSOCIATION FLOW

After years of various improv games, scenes, long forms, teaching new students, and noticing patterns in the collaboration and idea generation, I eventually developed a new approach to playing "What are you doing?" Again, there's a fun, competitive element to this game with a sort of "king of the hill" model, or like a scene from 1994 with that one person commanding the *Street Fighter 2* arcade machine while competitors line up to challenge them. Once I discovered this new approach, I found that I could keep going in the game, keep generating idea after idea, while others would eventually blank or stumble. Granted, this is one of thousands of games, and any real improviser will tell you that no one cares how good you are at a silly exercise. But the technique I call *association flow* goes way beyond a single game, and it started to permeate all of my improv, writing, performing, and innovation—it became a core approach to any creative endeavor.

In practice, here's what association flow looks like:

Association FLOW

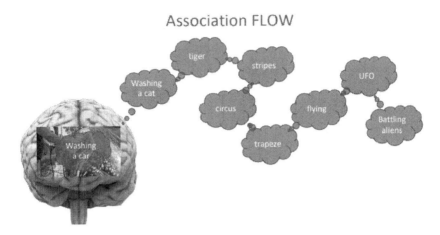

From "washing a car," we think of washing a cat, which at first is still within that "association orbit" mode. But from there, instead of pinging back to the first suggestion, we leap from the cat to tigers to stripes to circus... all the way to "battling aliens." This is a brief example, but once you start working your creative muscles with association flow, your brain can soon zip through a dozen association pings in a few seconds until you're making supposedly "random" leaps almost instantly. The outcome of the leap is not the point, though. We're just doing reps.

In *The Neuroscience of Creativity*, professor of neurophysiology Anna Abraham highlights improvisation as a *process-to-brain* phenomenon.[xxxiii] That is, rather than hope for the genetic advantage of Mozart or Einstein to lend you the *brain-to-process* advantage, starting with the process first can influence your brain, and that gradual rewiring can then improve the process. This is related to *neuroplasticity*, or the changes within your brain across your lifetime in response to deliberate learning and embodied experience.

If creativity is a muscle, association flow is your workout.

But before I assign you a practice for association flow that you can incorporate anywhere, let's take it up a level.

GRATITUDE FLOW

Okay, I get it: Practicing gratitude has become the overstuffed Pier One pillow of personal development, something you bookmarked and forgot about in 2017 after your mom heard about it on Oprah's podcast. But hear me out—or better yet, listen to David Whyte:[xxxiv]

> Gratitude is not a passive response to something we have been given. Gratitude arises from paying attention, from being awake in the presence of everything that lives within and without us. Gratitude is not necessarily something that is shown after the event; it is the deep, a priori state of attention that shows we understand and are equal to the gifted nature of life.

Your creative calling starts with your state of attention, and gratitude is a dominant driver for where your attention goes. Research shows that gratitude releases hormones such as dopamine and serotonin and regulates the sympathetic nervous system, mitigating motivation, mood and focus. Robert Evans, known as the world's leading scientific expert on gratitude, conducted studies with his team that found a host of physical, psychological, and social benefits from a regular gratitude practice.[xxxv] These included:

- A stronger immune system
- Better sleep

- Increased energy and alertness
- Being more outgoing
- More connection to others
- Less loneliness and isolation

This all sounds promising, but weren't we in the middle of a chapter about improvisation and creativity? It all comes together with *gratitude flow*.

Starting with the association flow model, we now incorporate gratitude and consider all the people connected to our lives—and by connected, I mean distantly connected, in ways you probably never even consider.

As we've just seen with the research, bringing in gratitude means this is no longer just an intellectual exercise. Now it's emotional. With the right degree of focus, that emotion and all those dimensions of gratitude will *supercharge* your creativity muscles.

Let's say you actually are washing a car. Here's how you could use your current activity to drop into gratitude flow:

Gratitude FLOW

For each of these steps, you're reflecting on someone or something required for your current action, possession, or reflection to exist. If you're washing your car, you can offer gratitude for an assembly worker who helped create your car. Or, as you see above, you can follow the flow, thinking of the breakfast the worker had that morning before stepping onto the assembly line, the farmer who collected the eggs for that breakfast, the watch that helped the farmer stay on schedule, the watchmaker who crafted that watch... all along the association flow until you're offering gratitude for a seamstress who mended a teddy bear.

Sound random? Perhaps, but the distinction between this process and an unstructured stream of consciousness is that you are deliberately and mindfully observing each turn, association, and leap, infusing each point with gratitude, and learning more about the inner workings of your inherent genius. You can practice Gratitude Flow at any time, simply observing your current activity, choosing an object as your springboard, and following the process. Over time, your senses sharpen, your connections quicken, and creativity feels less fleeting and more instinctive, grounded, and brimming with possibility.

MINIMUM VIABLE PRACTICE:
I NOTICE, I WONDER, WHAT IF...

George de Mestral was curious. Just home from a hunting trip, George pricked his fingers on the burs that covered his pants, then again when picking the persistent pieces of burdock plant from the fur of his Irish Pointer. He grabbed a handful of the burs and brought them into his office to place under his microscope. In that magnified light, he saw thousands of fibrous hooks, allowing the burdock to hitchhike along any passing fur or fabric. He also saw possibility.

Starting in 1941, George de Mestral began fashioning his synthetic versions of this hook-and-loop attachment, finally landing a patent in 1955 and ushering Velcro into production in the early '60s. Yes, you have George's moment of curiosity and persistence to thank for keeping your backpack latched and your kids' shoes attached.

This is one of many examples of innovation I cite when applying the improviser's mindset in a process I call *I Notice, I Wonder, What If...*

That ellipsis is doing most of the work.

This is a framework I first used when creating and facilitating an innovation course at Amazon. Used primarily in groups, I saw these simple prompts initiate breakthroughs in everything from product design to supply chain logistics. It's also another thought exercise you can try solo, either for a specific challenge or as another mental workout for your creative skills.

Take a challenge you're dealing with, something you're facing that customers also struggle with, or a creative project that has you up against a wall. Again considering how you are priming your attention for discovery, start by simply noticing.

- *I notice that these burs are stuck to my dog's fur...*
- *I notice that delivery routes are taking 20% longer than expected...*
- *I notice that my screenplay's resolution seems forced...*

As we did by turning from forced effort to gratitude, take a page from another personal development couplet: *Don't get furious, get curious.*

- *I wonder what causes these burs to stick...*
- *I wonder how we can make the routes more efficient...*
- *I wonder what I can set up to make the payoff more natural...*

For the last lever in your springboard sequence, put your curiosity to the test:

- *What if I can recreate these hooks synthetically...*
- *What if we replaced all the drivers with robots...*
- *What if I foreshadowed the resolution here...*

From "What if..." you can merge this practice into any brainstorming practice or solo exploration, taking notes without judgment until one of the ideas tugs on your intuition and pulls you into a new dimension of innovation and possibility. You may not invent the next Velcro, but each time you practice this process you're adding another creativity-building circuit to your mental workout.

WHOA THERE: OVERTHINKING AND UNDERDOING OR OVERDOING AND UNDERTHINKING?

In one of my favorite improv books, legendary improvisers Will Hines and Billy Merritt identify three broad categories of improvisers:

- **Robot:** The improviser who excels at logical connections and noticing patterns, but may struggle with emotional and physical immersion.
- **Pirate:** The improviser who swings into the scene and runs on instinct, fully embodied and emotional, though sometimes misses the structure and patterns that keep a story cohesive.
- **Ninja:** A hybrid of the robot and the pirate, the ninja starts as smoke and possibility, then merges into steel and resolve, then back again, finding both the emotional

thrust of the scene and the logical structure of the story. The ninja transforms depending on what's needed.[xxxvi]

The book that explains this framework is called *Pirate Robot Ninja: An Improv Fable*. Most improvisers aspire to be ninjas, and most will admit that they sometimes play into robot or pirate tendencies to a fault. (Big surprise, I'm a bit of a robot, though I have my ninja moments.)

As we apply improv to self-awareness, I find wisdom and inspiration from Hines and Merritt, as they provide a cautionary tale to our embrace of spontaneity as a cure-all. Do you ever find yourself in robot mode, stuck in analysis paralysis? Or, do you sometimes feel swept up and surging into pirate mode, following every drive and instinct without pause for reflection?

When theorizing about creativity, we also have the classic admonishment from E.B. White: "Explaining a joke is like dissecting a frog. You understand it better but the frog dies in the process." This has been one of my biggest weaknesses: Halting my flow by analyzing a story, poem, or scene as I'm creating it—dissecting the frog in mid-leap. For the sake of my career and the premise of this book, I still maintain that creativity can include and transcend analysis, as long as we have a way to "forget all that shit and play."

BALANCING ACT: SECOND NAÏVETÉ

> *Before studying Zen, mountains are mountains and waters are waters; after an insight into the truth of Zen through the instruction of a good master, mountains are not mountains and waters are not waters; but after attaining the abode of rest, mountains are once more mountains and waters are waters.*
> —Seigen Ishin

Creatives can be a superstitious lot. Chasing fickle inspiration, we're cautious of forcing insights or overthinking solutions. We'd prefer if every creative breakthrough arrived fully formed and unavailable for questioning, as if the Muse crashed through a skylight, handed us a solution, and then rushed past us down the courthouse stairs in a trench coat and sunglasses, her lawyers swatting away our requests as she slips into a black SUV and speeds away.

How do we interrogate creativity without exhausting the mystery? The French philosopher Paul Ricoeur wondered the same about spirituality, offering the frame of *second naïveté*, which other theorists have carried forward to apply to countless secular and creative works.[xxxvii]

One of my philosophy professors described second naïveté as the culmination of an inward spiral:

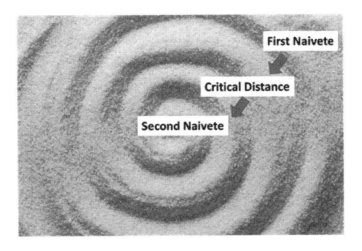

On the edge of the spiral, with *first naïveté*, we accept the mysteries as given, including any superstitions we inherit to explain their origin. In time, we move into the spiral as we apply critical distance, using scientific inquiry and skepticism to pick apart the source of wonder. You can see in the image that we appear to be in a sort of maze, or perhaps within a wheel, wrapped around the axle. Ricoeur notices that this critical distance is necessary, but is also disenchanting, as it might distance us too much from the core inspiration of the divine—or in our case, of the creative (again, feel free to treat theology as merely the metaphor here).

Unlike first naïveté, *second* naïveté cannot be a blank slate or an unrung bell. The knowledge of critical distance still resides, and yet we've moved on to that unconscious competence where the knowing is in the doing. Mark Linsenmayer, co-host of the podcast *The Partially Examined Life*, responds to the theory of second naïveté with a soft bafflement, admitting that he doesn't see how you can simply step into this ideal state of knowing without overthinking.[xxxviii] Linsenmayer notes that "It sounds like it's a matter of being open to a certain kind of religious/mystical experience: putting your mind at peace, clearing it of thoughts, focusing on your senses, your breathing, all that jazz, as one would have to do perhaps to enjoy certain types of jazz or other music that doesn't obtrusively jump out and grab you ('catchy' music)."

And that brings us back to improvised jazz! See, give me enough space to riff on the research, and everything is connected. The point of the theory is never to memorize a bunch of studies, authors, games, and frameworks. The point is how these exercises work your creative muscles. You don't need to carry the weights out of the gym to see the results.

That said, if you're still a bit woozy from the trip through our inward spiral, perhaps it's time to step back and settle our thoughts. Let's explore the creative insights and self-awareness of practicing mindfulness.

Chapter 4
Naked in a Stranger's Dining Room—Meditation, Mindfulness, and the Imperfect Path

Almost everything will work again if you unplug it for a few minutes, including you.
—Anne Lamott

In the tradition of Zen parables, you might be expecting "naked in a stranger's dining room" to be a metaphor. I wish that were the case.

In 2009, between a bad breakup and my last year of grad school, I signed up for a 10-day Vipassana meditation retreat in Central Washington State. The deal was that I would spend 10 days in silence, with no reading, writing, or breakdancing (I assume no breakdancing, but I didn't ask) for the entire stay. It was a communal retreat of all-day meditations, waking up each morning at 5 a.m. to meditate in our rooms, then congregate in a small meditation hall for formal teachings and longer bouts of strict, silent meditation. Two days in, however, my back was in constant spasms and I was struggling to breathe through the mucous mask of a summer cold. I met with one of the volunteer Vipassana coordinators and explained my plight before silently and shamefully shuffling out of the side door and driving home.

Still, I had eight days left in my vacation and a deadline to reach enlightenment before I returned to worldly things. I stayed off the email and social media grid, bought a book on Vipassana, watched a YouTube documentary about prisoners on a meditation retreat, and tried to manage my own haphazard retreat for one.

After three days of that, I got restless. *Isn't there a shortcut? I thought. Like, a hack?* In my Seattle apartment, I could still hear the traffic, still see my bills piling up, still trip over the ghosts of failed projects and ex-girlfriends and every rumination I had grafted onto my familiar surroundings. What I needed was to see and hear and feel less. What I needed was sensory deprivation.

In case you've never seen the Netflix series *Stranger Things*, a sensory deprivation tank is typically a sealed dark container of body-temperature water filled with salt. The idea is that you lie down in this space and let your body merge with the water, not hearing or seeing anything, until your mind unlatches from its constant onslaught of stimulation and allows you to float into an inky nothingness.[14] These days, you can't go four blocks in downtown Seattle without passing a sensory deprivation clinic, but at the time I could only find one local option online. When I reached out via email to schedule an appointment, I received a cryptic response: "Sorry, we're closed forever. Try this phone number." Sensing that I was being sent on some sensory deprivation mystic quest, I called the number. A distracted-sounding guy answered and said, "What? No. Oh, wait, I mean sure. Come to this address and bring $60 cash... yep, okay, thanks, bye."

---

[14]   And for the super advanced, you can astral project and fight demons with your mind.

So with that, I–"Oh, wait, are you still there?" said the guy on the phone. "Also bring a towel."

So... With that completely normal and non-sketchy exchange, I drove to this stranger's Bellevue house with cash and a towel and a dream of all my senses vanishing into an ethereal abyss. When I arrived, the man from the normal phone conversation answered the door: A mid-forties white guy with dreadlocks I'll call Kyle. "Namaste," he said (probably). Just then, two naked toddlers came screaming through the hallway. "Oh, don't mind them," said Kyle. "I just have them for the weekend but their mom is coming to pick them up in a few minutes." I stood there holding my towel and nodding, wondering about the difference between a smile and a grimace.

Kyle directed me to the shower, which was just past a mounted sex-swing and a collection of yoga mats piled like cord wood. He explained that I had to be completely clean and completely naked to enter the deprivation tank. After a quick lather of apricot scrub and a cold rinse, I wandered back out into his hallway with the towel around my waist, readier than ever for my senses to be deprived.

"The tank is just over here, in the mindfulness room," beckoned Kyle. I followed him around the corner to his "mindfulness room," which also resembled a cluttered dining room with a large white pod where a dining table should be.[15] Across from the pod was a cramped kitchen with a stack of dishes on the counter and a sink slowly dripping into an empty can of Heinz baked beans. Kyle opened the pod door and introduced me to my journey.

---

[15]   *I'm in the mindfulness room! I'm in the dining room! I'm in the combination mindfulness and dining room!*

Inside the pod, it was as dark as advertised. Feeling around, I found two small pool noodles to act as bumpers for my float, plus a third noodle as a neck pillow. The trouble was—and I cannot for the life of me fathom why—*I just could not relax.* The salty water splashed up into my mouth and eyes. Meanwhile the pod was not soundproof, so I could still hear the dripping sink filling up the can 'o beans a few feet away. I may have been deprived of my shirt and pants and $60 cash, but my senses were still firing on full alert.

Three minutes (?) in, I opened the hatch and tapped out, clutching the towel and fumbling for my pants.

"Oh, that's too bad," said Kyle. "You know, if you want I can get in there with you and try some massage techniques."

"Ope, no, that's very generous," I said. "But I'm good." My senses would need to be deprived another day.

THE IMPERFECT PATH

> *Instead of trying to tame the wild horses of thoughts and emotions inside a too-small corral, we simply open the gates, discovering the larger field of awareness in which the thoughts can move freely.*
> –Loch Kelly

Despite the occasional haphazard experiences in my enlightenment quest, I still find meditation to be an essential part of my daily practice. I've been meditating for over 25 years, taking up a simple sitting practice after reading Shunryu Suzuki's *Zen Mind, Beginner's Mind.* I identify as a Buddhist, and I sometimes incorporate mindfulness exercises in my coaching and facilitation, finding that clients and larger groups, even corporations, are becoming more open to the mainstream applications of meditation and the well-documented benefits, independent of belief.

I'm also a lousy meditator.

I add that caveat with its own sub-caveat (it's caveats all the way down), meaning that there's no such thing as a good or a bad meditator. You might be more or less disciplined, have a regular or sporadic practice, and have varying degrees of transcendence captured in your brain scans. But it's a joke to boast about being a great meditator, or to admonish yourself for feeling antsy or distracted when you try to sit and focus on your breath.

Oh, you keep losing track of your breath and get caught in your thoughts? That's the practice! We'll get more into a simple guidance for meditation in a moment, but for now, consider this: Saying that you can't meditate because you slip in and out of focus is like saying you can't lift weights because you keep putting them down. That activity, the flitting away and returning to the moment, represents your reps in mindfulness practice. That is how you fortify attention and presence—by recognizing when you're lost, but always returning.

Every other day you'll find another article touting the benefits of meditation. Rather than flood this chapter with every single claim and citation, I'll focus on a 2015 study published in *Nature*, documenting how meditation shapes the brain. Here's just a few highlights:

- Enhancing attention through development in the anterior cingulate cortex.
- Reducing stress and improving emotional regulation through engagement of the frontal-limbic networks.

- Deepening present moment awareness through the effects on the midline prefrontal cortex and posterior cingulate cortex in the Default Mode Network.[xxxix]

Aha! You knew the DMN was going to come back into the picture, didn't you? In previous chapters, we explored how the Default Mode Network is both vital for creativity as well as being hazardous, because it promotes rumination, but it doesn't feel like something you can directly control. If we return to the exercise metaphor (and embodiment is part of mindfulness), you could say that meditation is like strengthening your core, as every other movement extends from that center.

MINIMUM VIABLE PRACTICE:
SIT DOWN, BE HUMBLE

Whether or not you currently meditate, it always helps to return to a "beginner's mind" and consider the simplest practice. Here's one you can try for just 60 seconds. Seriously, read the instructions and then put the book down for one minute. Depending on your comfort and ability, you may adjust any elements to make this practice work for you:

1. Sit in an upright yet comfortable position.
2. Close your eyes and breathe through your nose.
3. Feel your body in this space, in this moment.
4. Starting with your toes and moving upward, notice any tensions in your body.
5. If you can, release those tensions, one by one.
6. Just sit.
7. Notice any thoughts that arise.

8. Don't try to change or eliminate the thoughts—just observe them like leaves flowing on a stream.
9. If your thoughts wander, just notice.
10. Return your focus to your breath.
11. Open your eyes.
12. Go to Audible and see if this book is available as an audiobook yet, because that would have made this sequence much easier.
13. If the audiobook isn't ready yet, give me some time. I'm recording the thing myself in this tiny booth in my guest room.
14. I mean, you'd think recording your own audiobook would come naturally, especially if you worked in radio for years.
15. But it's a TON of work.
16. Maybe send some mindful compassion to the author who is working so hard to get you enlightened, okay?
17. Now return to this space and just be present.
18. *Namaste*, probably.

See? Simple. There are many meditation practices, both guided and unguided, which you can find online or in one of the seven meditation apps you downloaded at some point and never opened.

Now that you know how to begin, here's one last tip: The moment you end the meditation, open your eyes, look around, and listen. Find a detail around you that you have never noticed, or noticed once and then shut out. It could be a single leaf outside your window, or the windchimes on your neighbor's porch. This exercise primes you to be startled back to life at any moment. After all, isn't that the first and last calling of any creative practice?

A 2014 study in *Frontiers of Psychology* breaks down different categories of meditation practice in a way that might shed light on the intersection between self-awareness and creativity.[xl] What we just reviewed is sometimes referred to as focused attention meditation, or FAM. In contrast, open monitoring meditation, or OMM, moves from a single point of focus to global awareness of whatever arises. The authors in *Frontiers* looked at studies that zeroed in on the brains of meditators in these different disciplines, finding that "OMM meditators outperformed FAM meditators when the target stimulus was unexpected." That is, those with the more singular focus may have been more locked in, but were less agile in shifting attention. "This might indicate that the OMM meditators had a wider attentional scope," add the *Frontiers* authors, "even though the two meditator groups did not differ in performance when the stimulus was expected."

What did you expect? If you meditate, do you notice how it primes your attention or shapes your creativity? If you don't meditate on a regular basis, do you think you could benefit from a deeper, singular attention or a more general awareness of your thoughts, feelings, and surroundings? The good news is that you don't have to choose. Just keep these categories in mind as you search for guided meditation practices, and give each approach a try. Take notes on your feelings and degrees of focus before and after the meditation.

At the heart of it all, mindfulness is deeply pragmatic. Meditation is not a strict, ascetic discipline; failure and imperfection are right there on the warning label. If you isolate the practice from spiritual connotations, at its core, meditation becomes purely an exercise that helps you stay mindful throughout the day. The instant you wake up, your brain is transitioning from the sleep state to the waking world. The consciousness and the unconsciousness in this state are like a heterogenous mixture of oil and water thrown into a blender—a walking, talking, complaining blender. Meditation as an exercise switches off the blender (which is your DMN on autopilot with sporadically firing circuits) and settles the sediment. When still, the soil settles at the bottom (the unconscious) and the water (consciousness) becomes clear. Once you have a clear distinction between your consciousness and your unconsciousness, you are no longer a highly-caffeinated blender, and it becomes easier to tap into the flow.

> *Then one afternoon...I realized that, actually, things were fine. Better than fine. I felt as though I had atomic vision. My attention was zingy; electric. I noticed everything—bap, bap, bap—flickers of intention before each movement, a vibrating topography of tensions and fluctuations under my belly skin, even my own keenly observant self. Such a good noticer. I noticed my ambition, my self-satisfaction, my disappointment that there was no one around to brag to about my progress ("You wouldn't believe how hard I can look at that tree").*
> —Dan Harris, *Meditation for Fidgety Skeptics*

WHOA THERE: CLIMBING BACK OUT OF YOUR MIND

Despite the hype, meditation is not a switch for instant enlightenment. Sometimes the process feels more like a detox, meaning that the issues you bring to the meditation might get worse before they get better. Ram Dass tells the story of a man who returned to his therapist after trying meditation for a few weeks. The man was indignant because he initially had a few bright moments, but his anxiety, anger, and sadness were getting worse. "What's going on?" he asked the therapist. "I thought you said meditation would make me feel better!"

"Yes," said the therapist. "Meditation makes you feel better. It makes you feel anxiety better, feel anger better, feel joy better..."

Wholeheartedness, through and through.

Even with meditation, high-performing creatives can take the practice overboard by striving too hard to do it "right," to be "enlightened," or blissful, or top of the transcendence leaderboards. I don't want to be one of those hipsters who says I started meditating before it was cool, but 25 years ago, we didn't have today's omnipresence of mindfulness products, "meditation hacks," and the marketing ploys that sometimes overpromise the reach of a simple practice–while also glossing over some of the psychological complexities that can surface. A 2022 study in the *Journal of Personality and Social Psychology* found that over-reliance on mindfulness meditation (one of many forms of meditation) can lead to an overly-inward focus and reduce our innate consideration for others.[xli]

Unsettling, perhaps, but you're not here to be settled. A part of us savors the backlash, as if meditation were this prim and unattainable character in a Victorian novel, just waiting to be taken down a notch. *Ohhh, look who has a dark side!*

If meditation can mitigate negative feelings, is it possible that we could lose touch with the natural signals to take proper action, responding to the sources of those feelings? An article in *Forbes* about the research put it this way:

The studies revealed that this short period of meditation reduced how guilty people felt, and this reduction in guilt went on to explain why people who meditated felt less motivated to pay back people they had harmed, compared to control condition participants (i.e., those who did not engage in the 10-minute meditation session).[xlii]

If we gathered a thousand researchers and a thousand meditators, we'd have a million perspectives about the real import of these observations.[16] Not getting too attached to the scientific conclusions, however, it's worth noting that the short-term "detox" period of meditation may require other modes of reflection to take you out of the inward spiral. Even in meditation, the areas you are stirring up and observing in the Default Mode Network can yank you right back onto the dance floor with your inner guard, rumination's *Greatest Hits* blasting on a persistent loop, including such memorable classics as:

- "I Don't Deserve to Be Here, Baby (Without Your Love)"
- "Never Good Enough to Get Down"
- "Jolene (Dolly Parton wrote Jolene and I Will Always Love You on the Same Day—Why Can't I Even Get Out of Bed?)"
- "I Want to Dance My Troubles Away, but One of My Troubles is I Can't Dance"

Snapping out of this trance is like becoming lucid in a dream. In your waking life, taking control sounds reasonable, but once

---

[16] Yes, somehow the two groups multiply each other; next-level imaginary math!

you've slipped into REM sleep, you find yourself again just playing the role your brain wrote out for you. So what does it take to wake up?

BALANCING ACT: RAIN AND LOVING KINDNESS

Meditation is to dive all the way within, beyond thought, to the source of thought and pure consciousness. It enlarges the container, every time you transcend. When you come out, you come out refreshed, filled with energy and enthusiasm for life.

–David Lynch

After college, I traveled to India for a few months and spent several weeks in a Tibetan monastery in Himachal Pradesh. For room and board, I taught English to the kids from the village and tutored one of the monks, using a novelization of *Babe, the Gallant Pig* as his reading guide. I also had the privilege of sitting with Lungtok Tenpai Nyima, also known as His Holiness The 33rd Menri Trizin.[xliii]

Until his passing in 2017, the 33rd Menri Trizin was head of the Tibetan Bon tradition, and a close contemporary of the Dalai Lama. In the monastery village of Dolanji, where I was staying, the Menri Trizin had a small home on the hillside. In my few meetings with him, I realized I wasn't ready or receptive to direct teaching. He laughed at my ramblings and told me I thought too much. I offered my theory on that. Then he loaned me a classic Tibetan text (translated into English) from his personal library. I read it patiently, but nothing got through.

Then, a week into my stay, a monsoon hit and everything changed. Heavy rains washed a boulder across the main village road, and the Menri Trizin walked down the hill from his home, spinning a yellow umbrella. He stopped to observe a group of monks lined up to break the boulder down.

Wait, do I have pictures of this somewhere? Oh, here you go:

The boulder was about seven feet in diameter, blocking over half the road, but the monks looked undaunted. One at a time, each monk would take turns sitting on top of the boulder, holding a large chisel. The next monk in line would then pick up a sledgehammer and swing away. With each swing, a tiny demolition of rock and dust exploded from the chisel point.

"Are you sure that will work?" I asked. "That looks like it will take forever."

The Menri Trizin looked over at me. He laughed and winked, then nodded at the monks, still swinging and chiseling.

Each day on my way to and from the classroom or the dining hall, I walked past the line of monks working on the boulder. Each day it looked a little smaller, but still impossible. Then, finally, about three weeks after the boulder first slid into the road, it was gone. Dust. The monks returned to their meditations and studies. I looked up the road and there was the Menri Trizin, spinning his yellow umbrella as he walked past.

"That's amazing!" I said. "The boulder is gone!"

"Gone?" he said. "Not gone, but gone." He laughed and kept walking.

"Did you rig that whole mudslide and boulder as an elaborate metaphor on my account?" I called back. "If so, that's a lot of work for a lesson!"

"You think too much!" he said without turning back.

RECOGNIZE, ALLOW, INVESTIGATE, NURTURE

As you can see in the photos, that was a real, non-metaphorical boulder. Still, the lesson felt transparent and embodied in a way I could never grasp from abstract wisdom. One day your mind feels clear, like walking down an open road lined by apple trees. Then suddenly you're caught in a monsoon of worries, doubts, frustrations, and fears, and a house-sized boulder of belief slides down to block your path. Taken in all it once, it feels impossible. But if you pick up the hammer, steady the chisel, or sit down to meditate, then with each swing, each breath, the boulder slowly drifts away. "Not gone, but gone." Matter and energy don't disappear—they transform. A wall of stone is now dust beneath your feet.

We all think too much. Mindfulness practice is not about eliminating thinking, but is rather about *transforming* it. The American psychologist and author Tara Brach recommends a system that she calls RAIN: Recognize, Allow, Investigate, Nurture. This process complements meditation by giving your worried mind an acronym and a checklist for any intrusive thought.

Let's test RAIN with the thought, "I'm an imposter."

- **Recognize what is happening inside and outside.** Note what triggered this thought, if anything, and observe it without judgment or resistance. Get curious, like an anthropologist for your brain. *Wow, my brain produced this thought. Fascinating.*

  ○ Also recognize what's happening in your body. Take a breath and scan for any tensions as you would during meditation. Where does this thought take residence? In your gut? Your chest? Your elbow would be a clever place to hide.

- **Allow the experience to take place and take shape.** You're giving space for this thought and the resident feelings to just observe and let the experience unfold. In this example, let these "imposter" feelings play out a bit, not identifying with them or resisting them, but witnessing with compassion.

- **Investigate with curiosity.** This is not an invitation to spiral into over-thinking, but just to lightly investigate or explore the thoughts and feelings arising. Gently question any assumptions behind the thought. *My brain must have a reference point for "I," whatever that is, and it thinks this term "imposter" is an accurate label.* Is that true? (If the instinctive reaction is "yes," add a dimension from Byron Katie: "Can I *absolutely* know that this is true?" Likely not.)

- **Nurture yourself based on what you have learned.** Stay compassionate. This is a delicate balance, because on one level you're observing, abstracting, and depersonalizing a bit, but as long as you can be with it, stay present and embodied.

RAIN is simple and profound, and it may take practice before it feels right. You may need to start the practice as part of your Morning Pages or other journaling, allowing time to observe, write, and let your self-reporting reveal what you otherwise missed. Using RAIN regularly, you will be well-equipped for another meditation practice to pull you out of the inward spiral. Like reps in martial arts, I find this practice primes my mind to respond differently in real time, instinctively dismantling those moments of external or internal pressure. Assumptions, judgments, or what once would have been the start of a spiral... they all become, as the Zen saying puts it, "like specks of snow falling onto a hot stove."

KINDNESS: I'M LOVING IT

In that same study on the limitations of mindfulness meditation, psychologist Andrew Hafenbrack recommends balancing your practice with "Loving Kindness" meditation.[17] Also known as "metta," loving kindness brings me back into that allocentric space and makes my creativity feel more expansive.

Allocentric is a wonky word, but I find it helpful. Allocentric lacks an easy synonym, though you're probably familiar with the antonym: *egocentric*. In this context, however, egocentric does not carry all of the Freudian baggage of being selfish or neurotic. It simply means "centered on the self," or starting a philosophical inquiry focused on the self and working outward from there. Meanwhile, as you might guess, allocentric is "focused on the other," in both interest and attention. With the egocentric and the allocentric, these twin stars of the psyche in an awkward teenage slow dance, we can consider how mindfulness and loving kindness operate between the self and other—neither superior nor inferior, but coordinating the ongoing balance between the two.

---

[17] Here's a guided loving kindness meditation to get you started: https://ggia.berkeley.edu/practice/loving_kindness_meditation

Loving Kindness meditation often starts, technically, as egocentric—sending goodwill toward yourself. For those struggling to develop self-compassion as a starting point, you can try this modification:

1. Start in a comfortable but attentive position.
2. Think first of someone dear to you who awakens unconditional love—perhaps a child.
3. With this person in mind, offer thoughts such as, "May you be happy. May you be loved. May you have peace."
4. Now imagine that person mirroring those same thoughts to you: "May you be happy. May you be loved. May you have peace."
5. Give yourself as much time as you need to truly feel those intentions.
6. Let the internal voice echo the loving kindness directed toward you and internalize it: "May I be happy. May I be loved. May I have peace."
7. Once you are filled with positive goodwill, imagine that you have more than enough within you to offer to others.

When you explore the deeper resources on loving kindness, such as those in the resource section of this book, you will find opportunities to go deeper, extending out to your neighbors, your community, to strangers you feel neutral about, and finally to those you might consider your "enemies," or sources of resentment.

I've heard from friends and clients that loving kindness meditation also inspired creative breakthroughs. This makes sense, as it aligns with your gratitude flow practice, flexes your imagination, and expands your mind's horizons.

Once you have a grounding practice, then, feeling clear and stable with a strong core, you're ready to enter another room in our mental gymnasium: The study and practice of philosophy.

Chapter 5
Hemlock and Key—Let's Make Our Brains Hurt with Some Philosophy

The point of philosophy is to start with something so simple as not to seem worth stating, and to end with something so paradoxical that no one will believe it.
—Bertrand Russell

"Okay, Jeremy, you'll have to give me a moment. You sort of broke my brain."

This was my first session with a client I'll call Mark. We had just come to the crux of a problem he was dealing with, choosing between selling his consulting agency or scaling it with a new partner. What's odd was not just that he said I "broke his brain;" what's odd, almost uncanny, is that I had heard something like this from a few clients before. They always mean it in a good way, and sometimes they have no idea what made everything *click* for them. I don't lecture or monologue, and most of what I do is ask seemingly simple questions. They sometimes wonder what sort of "trick" I was using to trigger the breakthrough.

Mind you, with these "brain breaking" moments, I'm not using Jedi mind tricks, hypnosis, or anything manipulative. I've helped clients unlock life-altering insights based on strategic questions that call out patterns and assumptions in how they think—not just on the surface, but digging past the layers of unexamined beliefs, choices, comparisons, habits, and views of the world. In short, the "trick" I'm using is philosophy.

For me, philosophy started as a joke. Quite literally, I cultivated my love of philosophy as a teenager while reading *The Hitchhiker's Guide to the Galaxy* novels by Douglas Adams. In this science fiction book series, scientists call upon a supercomputer called Deep Thought that designed and constructed the Earth. They ask this powerful machine to answer the "Ultimate Question of Life, The Universe, and Everything." After 7.5 million years of processing and calculation, Deep Thought answers "42." When asked what kind of answer that is, Deep Thought asks its interrogators to clarify the question.

So before we waste a few million years only to get a numeric punchline, let's clarify the questions of this chapter:

- Who are you?
- How did you get past the guards?[18]
- What drives you to create?
- What is the relationship between the "self" and creative work?

As Bertrand Russell would have it, these questions might sound "so simple as to not seem worth stating," which is why it makes them so insidious. Few of us love the mental equivalent of standing on firm ground only to have a Wile-E-Coyote moment, look down, and plummet into the valley below. We're

---

[18] By "guards" here, I mean the guards of societal convention, the guards of your mental filters… or something.

left to unflatten ourselves, dust off, and embark again on the endless chase for the "Roadrunner" of ultimate truth.

It's no coincidence that I discovered philosophy and improv around the same time. Both disciplines forced me to question assumptions and constantly reinvent who I was becoming. When I enrolled in philosophy courses at Gonzaga University, I was hooked. I remember my Ethics 101 class in the basement of the liberal arts building, taught by an eccentric Jesuit (redundant phrase) who had an odd obsession with Demi Moore. Fueled by the watery vanilla coffee from the vending machine, I scribbled lecture notes like, "HOW ARE WE TO LIVE?" It struck me as confounding that it took 18 years to start thinking about these basic questions in such a direct manner. Had I ever thought about how to live before, or was I on autopilot?

My junior year, I went on to play the central role of Arthur Dent in a stage production of *The Hitchhiker's Guide*, hamming it up with an affected accent that could be called "British" in the way that warm pond water could be called "tea." I loved it. Arthur and I shared many things in common: We were both constantly flummoxed, heartbroken, exasperated, easily pulled into the exploits of others, and eventually forced to reckon with our own fate and step into our cosmic accountability.

I suspected that philosophy had the answers I needed to find my place in the world. My formal studies and writing, however, led me into a classic pretentious phase. At 20 years old, filled with self-assurance that I had stumbled onto profound revelations, I asked my Demi-loving ethics professor to read my magnum opus. He gave me high marks on previous papers, and with my latest endeavor he was gracious to a point, but then he returned my paper a few days later with a beer mug ring on the cover, and on the second page he left a simple inscription in red ink: "I stopped reading here."

I don't blame him. If you read that old essay, you'd see how it plays into every cliché that scares most away from pure philosophy: dense, solipsistic, meandering, and brimming with unearned smugness. This was decades before *The Good Place* built on the legacy of *Hitchhikers* to make philosophy accessible, human, funny, sexy, and moving, and I wish I had that foresight to drop the pretense and connect my instincts of greater depths with an expansive series of revelations carried across four seasons of pure television gold.

Michael Schur, creator of *The Good Place*, also wrote a brilliant book cheekily titled *How to Be Perfect: The Correct Answer to Every Moral Question*. Schur shares how philosophy can make you more authentic, pointing to answers you might miss with modern shortcuts:

> The best thing about Aristotle's "constant learning, constant trying, constant searching" is what results from it: a mature yet still pliable person, brimming with experiences both old and new, who doesn't rely solely on familiar routines or dated information about how the world works.

Schur also independently makes the connection between philosophers and improvisers, which makes us best friends (he and his lawyers just don't understand that yet). While Schur is more focused on the thesis of his series, however, "what we owe to each other" through the lens of moral philosophy and giant lava demons, here I'm exploring a different inquiry: What can philosophy tell you about who you are and what you create?

Whether you're talking about philosophy or art, one commonality stands: Your parents "did not invest their life savings in your education to pursue a degree in this." Should you blame them? Try justifying a graduate degree in cultural studies, where they somehow let me get away with writing a musical about Friedrich Nietzsche as my capstone.[19] That said, the easy punchlines undermining both creative and philosophical lives capture only a distorted commentary. Both art and philosophy, though, can provoke similar levels of distrust, with casual observers feeling overwhelmed, intimidated, or patronized. They would rather roll up the entire enterprise into an easy caricature and dismiss it as pretentious than admit that they don't understand it.

Yes, philosophy can be dry, boring, and infuriating, but with the right curation and commentary, it can also offer us more wisdom per square inch than any breezy personal development guide. With thousands of years of development (compared to psychology starting as a formal discipline in the late 19th century), philosophy provides the hidden origins of many contemporary, watered-down ideas we now take for granted. Philosophy is a source code beneath it all. For example, my whole framework of the *minimum viable practice*, *overdoing it*, and *the balancing act* is a loose bastardization of Aristotle's golden mean—finding the right center between too little or too much of a given virtue.

For creatives, philosophy can also offer us rigor, structure, depth, and yes, even imagination to explore our inner lives, our relationships to others, and how our beliefs, values, and assumptions shape the world around us. To return again to the "mental workout" metaphor, I've often considered applied psychology and personal development to be a sort of cardio, while mindfulness offered mobility and flexibility, and philosophy provided the heavy lifting.

Ready for some deadlifts?

---

[19]   I wrote the book and lyrics; the brilliant Rob Scherzer wrote the music.

PHILOSOPHY AS COUNTERWEIGHT

Philosophy is the struggle against the bewitchment
of our minds by means of language.
–Ludwig Wittgenstein

In musicals, characters break into song when a feeling is so overwhelming that they can't express it in speech. Every creative feels an equivalent brimming over that drives our work, knowing that our direct and unadorned expressions can only capture a fraction of our lived experience. That is, if every human connection required us to be as direct as possible, to always say exactly what we mean and "explain it like I'm five," then we'd all have the same beautiful innocence and limitations of five-year-olds. We'd still be full of emotion and energy, but unable to convey life's complexity with any depth or nuance.

But in our artistic answers to overwhelming feelings, we also have the tendency to be a bit *extra*. If we let creative impulse rule not just our art, but also our boundaries of emotional regulation, we lose all points of reference. What use is the perfect sonnet, sculpture, or symphony when you can't get out of bed, manage your finances, or focus on anything longer than a TikTok?

Meanwhile, will philosophy be so dry that it robs us of our creative spirit? In college, I complained to my friend Brett that all the Plato and Kant and Hume I was reading was making my improv too heady and less spontaneous. "Check out Nietzsche," Brett said. "His book *The Birth of Tragedy* made me a better guitar player." How was that possible? Brett never elaborated, but I heard him play Van Morrison's "Brown Eyed Girl" at a party once, and he was good. Maybe there was something to *Nietzsche* after all.

In *The Birth of Tragedy*, Friedrich Nietzsche explores the balancing forces of order and chaos through the warring values of Apollo and Dionysus. To oversimplify, Apollo represents order, temperance, and restraint, while Dionysus brings the revelry of passion, dancing, debauchery, and ecstasy. If you received party invites from both Apollo and Dionysus, it's a no-brainer which would have a line out the door. Still, while the Dionysian party might be epic, the revelers might also set your house on fire and fill your swimming pool with tequila if they're not kept in check by the buzzkill of Apollonian order. We need both the pure lifeforce of inspiration and the structure of rulesets to balance meaning and expression.

If I read nothing but poetry, fiction, and drama, at some point I have to put it down for a while, if only because it isn't meeting my need for a balanced reading list, to have at least one *process*-oriented book—dense, rational, cohesive.

I can't imagine sustaining on poetic logic alone. If my convictions arrived the way my poetry did, I'd be lost. I'd be pleased and utterly seduced, but lost. Homeless. Where is the accountability in poetic conclusions? *Should* poems conclude anything, or should they remain provisional by nature? All our concepts of consciousness, morality, identity, behavior, cause and effect, are shaped at least in part by metaphor—even the strictest mathematical logic relies on analogy. But the process-oriented methods still answer to structures, tests, and empirical landscapes. By contrast, Jorie Graham observes:

> Poetry can also be difficult, though, because much of it attempts to render aspects of experience that occur outside the provinces of logic and reason, outside the realm of narrative realism. The ways in which dreams proceed, or magic,

or mystical vision, or memory, are often models for poetry's methods: what we remember upon waking, what we remember at birth—all the brilliant Irrational in the human sensibility. Poetry describes, enacts, is compelled by those moments of supreme passion, insight or knowledge that are physical yet intuitive, that render us whole, inspired. Among verbal events—which by their nature move horizontally, through time, along the lines of cause and effect—poetry tends to leap, to try to move more vertically: astonishment, rapture, vertigo—the seduction of the infinite and the abyss—what so much of it is after.[xliv]

There's something here to the way we receive rhetoric, conflating seductive phrasing with well-tempered arguments. The more charming politician is more popular, whether their citations are empty or not. The poem more sympathetic to our cause expects more praise, whether it is well-crafted or not. These are the surface conclusions of popular culture, naturally drawing suspicion from the more attentive audience, but still hard to get around.

How do we do it, then? How do we separate tenability from sensuous phrasing? Then there's the notion that poetry transcends logic, that its instincts are deeper, closer to the marrow, covered in soot and soil and more spontaneous, more embodied and present than any empirical process. In this manner, poetry often resides in stillness, the poet in chaos. I mean, I can't blame them: It's a damn soothing rhetoric we create, those who know the cadence of wisdom, but not the heart.

A PHILOSOPHICAL TASTING MENU

Now I will breeze through two millennia of Western and Eastern philosophies in a few paragraphs. Or, more practically, let's rush through the halls of these vaunted academic traditions, knock some shit over, and ransack whatever looks useful. Let's be recklessly selective and just skim over a few choice samples of wisdom that happen to suit our immediate needs. For you philosophy geeks and academics, I apologize now for everything I'm about to overlook, but I want to give you just a taste of a few philosophical traditions, looking specifically at our questions of the authentic self and creativity.

Stoicism: *Do You Even Memento Mori, Bro?*

> *People say: 'What good does it do to point out the obvious?' A great deal of good; for we sometimes know facts without paying attention to them. Advice . . . merely engages the attention and rouses us, and concentrates the memory, and keeps it from losing its grip. We miss much that is set before our eyes.*
> –Seneca

Ah, Stoicism. It's not just the bro philosophy your cousin Dale posts about with Seneca quotes over his Instagram deadlifts. In recent years, Stoicism has enjoyed a revival, as many authors have penned popularized commentaries on the Stoic insights into self-awareness, resilience, courage, and discipline. Stoicism also provided the "source code" for cognitive behavioral theory, which we touched on earlier, as this school of thought remains duly practical for navigating our modern anxieties. That said, be careful not to confuse Stoicism with our contemporary use of the lowercase "stoic," meaning indifferent or sometimes numb to pleasure and pain. The original Stoics did value resolve and reason in the face of extreme emotion, but their full philosophy was much more varied and robust.

In *The Philosophy of Cognitive Behavioral Therapy*, psychotherapist and philosopher Donald Robertson reassures us that philosophy is not meant to be an outdated academic exercise, but rather the fierce pursuit of a "warrior of the mind:"

> For Socrates and the Stoics, the notion that the goal of human life is the pursuit of wisdom does not equate to saying that the 'meaning of life' is that one should spend it reading books on philosophy, but, rather, that one should strive for practical wisdom in facing everyday challenges.

If you've ever taken solace in the "serenity prayer," you have the Stoics to thank for the source code. Usually attributed to theologian Reinhold Niebuhr, this prayer calls for a higher force to "grant me the serenity to accept the things I cannot change, the strength to change the things I can, and the wisdom to know the difference." In this framework, we can see direct influence from the Stoics, who placed great value in self-awareness, including a certain degree of surrender to forces larger than ourselves. Put simply by Epictetus, "Some things are up to us and others are not."

Taking a philosophical lens to imposter syndrome, how much of your self-doubt is due to your actions, and how much is a projection of the perceptions of others? Can you fully control what others think about you? You want to perform well, act virtuously, treat others well, and be your authentic self, but as we've discussed, the "imposter" label is based on a leap in logic beyond the bounds of your actions. The Stoics might also ask why you give so much credence to the imaginary judgments of others. In the words of Roman Emperor and Stoic Marcus Aurelius, seek out "the tranquility that comes when you stop caring what they say, or think, or do. Only what you do."

Author Ryan Holliday notes that Marcus Aurelius himself had a form of imposter syndrome, feeling unworthy of being emperor when compared to his predecessor Antonius Pius.[xlv] Reportedly breaking into tears over his self-doubt, you can imagine Marcus calling himself "the poor man's Pius," "discount Antonius," or "definitely not to be as revered and remembered as Antonius, who centuries from now everyone will know better than Marcus and definitely not have to look up Antonius on Wikipedia and go, *Huh, I didn't know about that guy*."

Meanwhile, to those close to you, those who really see you and support you, could you ever be an imposter? From *The Daily Stoic* podcast, Ryan Holliday cites Steven Pressfield:

> I don't think there really is such a thing as being an imposter. You're just on the spectrum of getting better and getting better. But I do think that we're sort of led to a calling or to something that we do. The trick to me is self-belief. It's just believing that you are not an imposter. Who says you're an imposter? That's the voice of resistance in your head, trying to sabotage you... You're being called in some sort of way like a dream is calling you or like you're unconscious or the muse or whatever you wouldn't be given that... unless you were capable of somehow enacting it.[xlvi]

The Stoics on Creativity

Among the other virtues that rise above criticism, Marcus Aurelius also considered the unconditional worth of beauty:

Does anything genuinely beautiful need supplementing? No more than justice does – or truth, or kindness, or humility. Are any of those improved by being praised? Or damaged by contempt? Is an emerald suddenly flawed if no one admires it?

Beyond natural beauty, what would the Stoics say about the beauty we create through art? Does creativity serve a greater purpose, or only offer distraction and leisure? Seneca himself wrote 10 tragedies, each of them an exploration of character, morality, and the difficult choices we are forced to make to live a meaningful life. Seneca also didn't object to a little diversion, noting that "Cato used to refresh his mind with wine after he had wearied it with application to affairs of state, and Scipio would move his triumphal and soldierly limbs to the sound of music."

In enjoying and creating art, you are not only providing sources of joy, you are offering your unique dimensions of meaning, which in turn may help others to flourish and create and knock over coffee tables as they dance in Dionysian revelry. While the lowercase "stoic" might bristle at art's excess, the true Stoic would admire someone who creates more than consumes, who makes an impact on the world by showcasing their passions and skills.

Plato and Socrates: The Original Matrix

Alfred North Whitehead once remarked that all Western philosophy was a "footnote to Plato." While this statement probably led Alfred's friends to refer to him as "Captain Overstatement," many philosophy pundits love to cite this quote to justify their seventy-fifth rereading of *The Republic*.

Socrates was arguably the first known Western philosopher from Athens, Greece, though he authored no works of philosophy or literature. All his theories and teachings were documented by his students, including Plato. In Plato's *Republic*, he depicts Socrates in a long series of debates about the true meaning of justice and human nature. Most famously, Socrates explains the plight of limited human perspectives through the "Allegory of the Cave," describing a group of people chained in a dark cave from birth with no reference to the outside world. They are forced to face the back wall of the cave and they can't even turn around. Behind them is a fire, and between them and the fire is a walkway. On the walkway, people go about their daily commutes, paying no heed to the creepy allegorical cave. Some walk with animals, others with musical instruments, and others with puppets representing people. All that the prisoners can see are the shadows cast on the wall of the cave.

What would happen if a prisoner broke free? wonders Socrates. *What if that freed prisoner saw the real world and rushed back to inform the prisoners?* Socrates and his companions then play out the hypothetical situation, considering how much people love to be proven wrong. The conclusion? The other prisoners would be so conditioned and attached to their perceptions that they would sooner kill the free man then change their worldview. Bleak, sure, but darkly satisfying in a *Black Mirror* sort of way.

Naturally, there's much more to Plato's argument, and the entire text of *The Republic* is surprisingly accessible, engaging, and even funny at times. Then again, you can just trust that I perfectly captured every nuance of this classic text. I just received a call from the Society for Platonic Studies to announce they are replacing all of Plato's original texts with my glib summary. You're welcome.

In applying the lessons of Plato's cave, there's a danger of slipping into *Dunning-Kruger* territory. If you identify as the freed prisoner trying to wake up all the "sheeple," you and your art become preachy and arrogant. If, however, you consider the humbling lessons of perceptions and limited worldviews, you might question the knee-jerk conclusions provided by your inner guard. Just because a thought casts its shadow, should you embrace it as your only reality? What would happen if you broke free from this darkness and sought the source of light? In the words of my college roommate, *at least open the blinds*.

The "Allegory of the Cave" has famously influenced films such as The *Matrix* and *The Truman Show*, each featuring a hero breaking through the illusion of their perceived world. In the HBO series *Westworld*, the robots appearing human frequently talk about "questioning the nature of your reality." There's something resonant with imposter syndrome here, that itch or instinct that *something's not quite right*. But for any of these characters, that unease is what propelled them to take charge, sail off, dodge bullets, and create new worlds. Where would they be if they had been perfectly content? In a boring story, that's where.

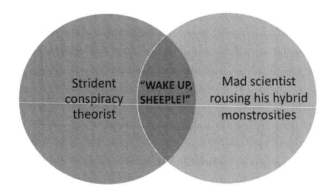

Existentialism: No Beret Required

She throws herself into things with ardor, because she is
not yet deprived of her transcendence; and the fact that she
accomplishes nothing, that she is nothing, will make her
impulses only the more passionate. Empty and unlimited,
she seeks from within her nothingness to attain All.
　　　　　　　　　　　　　　　　　—Simone de Beauvoir

Here's another way that philosophy made me super fun and popular in school: When someone asked about my astrological sign, I would say, "I'm an existentialist."

"That's not a sign," they'd reply.

"Exactly," I'd say. "It means I believe I control my own fate and don't rely on the superstitions of star alignments and birthdays."

At this point, the other person would back away slowly, find the nearest window, and determine if they could survive a quick self-defenestration.

To be fair to 20-year-old me, there is some merit in taking responsibility for your actions beyond uncontrollable forces. Just don't, you know, be a jerk about it.

Existentialists like Jean-Paul Sartre, Albert Camus, and Simone De Beauvoir would have a field day with the notion of "imposter syndrome."[20] Each hitting their prime in the 1930s and '40s, this trio represented the most famous thinkers in the existentialist tradition, and they each wrote at length about what it means to be authentic, enact free will, act justly in an unjust world, and of course, smoke and laugh and fight and make love and drink apricot cocktails until daybreak. By all accounts, these philosophers knew how to party.

---

[20]　As would Nietzsche, who is sometimes referred to as a "proto-existentialist."

More than pleasure, though, the existentialists were preoccupied with *meaning*. As opposed to the *essentialism* of classic philosophy, assuming that we are all imbued with some divine, innate purpose, Sartre insisted that "existence precedes essence," which called on each of us to define our purpose and forge the courage to follow it. "Freedom," said Sartre, "is what we do with what is done to us."

If this sounds somewhat liberating so far, then why does existentialism have a reputation for being such a bummer? Sartre said that we are "condemned to be free," acknowledging that there's a heavy burden in identifying your purpose, following your purpose, trying not to follow your purpose too closely, ducking behind a tree when your purpose turns around to see if you're following it, and explaining to the judge that the restraining order isn't necessary because you are destined to follow your purpose and you're not a purpose stalker, you swear.

That's not exactly how Sartre put it, but he's basically saying it's a lot of work.

In her dazzling intellectual history *At the Existentialist Café*, Sarah Bakewell summarized Sartre's insights on the provisional nature of the self:

> You might think you have defined me by some label, but you are wrong, for I am always a work in progress. I create myself constantly through action, and this is so fundamental to my human condition that, for Sartre, it is the human condition, from the moment of first consciousness to the moment when death wipes it out. I am my own freedom: no more, no less.

Without inherent purpose, we face absurdity. That is, not the surreal absurdity of Andre Breton's "horse galloping on a tomato," but the existential absurdity of expecting answers from a world that owes you nothing. This resembles comic or artistic absurdity because the existentialists are laughing into the void, observing that life makes no sense, or doesn't "mean" anything except through the meaning we give it. Though Friedrich Nietzsche predated the existentialists by a few decades, some consider him a "proto-existentialist" for his call to create meaning for ourselves, ultimately (despite his reputation) to overcome nihilism by becoming "the poet of our lives."

This is the theme that many miss when mislabeling Nietzsche as a nihilist or assuming the existentialists were deeply pessimistic. It's as if some commentators read half the book, sighed deeply, looked outside at the crows gathering in the trees, and fell asleep.

Let's not make the same mistake. While Camus grappled with the question of suicide as "the only serious philosophical question," he also gave us this: "In the depths of winter, I found there was, within me, an invincible summer." When Camus entreated us to "live and create" and "live to the point of tears," he invoked an authentic, artistic life aligned with Richardson's choral feelings, where "every glass in the cupboard sings."

Existentialism is often considered dour, but Sartre claimed that he had never felt a day of despair. Sartre and the other existentialists were vocal about the horrors of war, genocide, famine, the corruption of political institutions, and the feelings of isolation and hopelessness against the tide of history. But they didn't succumb to a passive cynicism. To shake your head and say, "That's a shame, but nothing can be done" would constitute "bad faith," in Sartre's terms, because it assigns meaning to an uncaused force and threatens to absolve you of a meaningful response to injustice, inequality, loss, or failure.

For the existentialists, the most meaningful response was often creativity. Sartre, Camus, and Beauvoir all wrote novels, giving their philosophies more accessible entry points for public consumption, and also illustrating the need for imagination to address absurdity. In Sartre's novel *Nausea*, the character Roquentin has a moment where he touches a seat on a train, only to feel suddenly disoriented by the nature of this plain object—its place, purpose, and design—and he seems to see it with fresh eyes. Roquentin feels a sort of liberating terror in this moment, because it's not about the seat on the train, but rather about all the moments of his daily life that he takes for granted or walks past in a trance. Here both the artist and the philosopher practice that Zen mantra, "Always unfamiliar!" As with gratitude flow, any object or action presents an opportunity to pause, reflect, strip away assumptions, and discover new depths.

Meanwhile, tracing the burden of freedom to a grand political scale, Simone de Beauvoir's World War II-era novel *The Blood of Others* places her characters at the crux of impossible moral choices. When you witness suffering, what are your obligations to intervene? How much should you sacrifice? If meaning is what you make of it, how can you measure the worth of your life or legacy? Beauvoir answers each of these questions neatly and definitively.

I'm kidding. There are no clear answers. She breaks our hearts, guts us, makes us dizzy with philosophical uncertainty, and leaves us to sort out the lessons for our own lives, if we wish to reduce the novel to practical applications.

If morality and meaning are inherited constructions, then, what does that say about your sense of self? If you think you're an imposter, that implies a "true" self you're neglecting. The existentialists would challenge you to investigate how your upbringing, beliefs, personality, and projections are all attached to some trusted authorities—either other people or the authorities of belief systems. What would happen if you, like Roquentin, stepped back from the object of "self" with a feeling of liberating terror? It sounds heavy, but that terror gives the question its charge and impact. Making it a mild thought experiment wouldn't do the trick.

For all of their drama and mind fuckery, the existentialists ultimately offer us consolation, because they show us that uncertainty is a feature and not a bug. A static sense of self would serve no one. Unbridled confidence would become boorish, and any art drawn from certainty would be predictable, stale, and probably smell like a haze of Axe body spray and shots of vodka and Red Bull.

I'd prefer apricot cocktails any day.

MINIMUM VIABLE PRACTICE: QUESTION YOUR INNER GUARD

> *It's not what is happening in your mind that matters; it's how you relate to it.*
> –Joseph Goldstein

Return to your inner dialogue. When you succumb to self-doubt, you're granting authority to your inner guard, because that voice takes advantage of negativity bias and fear to dampen your inherent courage.

One coaching client recently told me how his self-doubt clashes with all the praise he hears from his own clients.

"What does your inner guard say?" I asked.

"It says, 'You have no business doing this. You're not helping anyone,'" he reported.

"What do your clients say?"

"They say, 'Your work is incredible. You totally transformed my life.'"

"Which opinion do you believe more?"

"My clients."

"Why is that?"

He laughed. "Because I'm a terrible judge of my own worth."

And yet here he was, giving his inner guard a pass because he assumed those thoughts were magically more credible than the rest of his "terrible judgment."

I didn't press him on the self-criticism about his own judgment, but you can see how we're entering a hall of mirrors here, *doubting the source of doubt.*

What would happen if your inner guard suddenly doubted all these thoughts about doubt? A head trip, I know, but that's exactly the point. You're taking trips inside your head all day, only to find that these epic, exhausting journeys are tracing the same spot on the carpet in repetitive circles.

Take a page from Socrates and get curious with your inner guard. Ask open-ended questions. Psychologists call this process "Socratic," or "dialectic," uncovering false beliefs with good-faith curiosity. Write out your back-and-forth to trace the exchange, and spot the holes in the logic and the thinking traps identified by CBT. It might look something like this:

Inner Guard (IG): "I don't think you're good enough to audition for this role."

You: "Interesting. Tell me how you identify 'good enough.'"

IG: "Simply being better than the others auditioning."

You: "And who are these others? Do you know all of them?"

IG: "Well, not all, but The World's Greatest Actor will probably show up."

You: "Let's say you're right, and if the casting director has to choose between me and The World's Greatest Actor, by what measure would you say I'm 'not good enough' in comparison?"

IG: "By... Well, it's just a feeling."

You: "By 'feeling,' you mean fear?"

IG: "Yes. I'm afraid."

You: "That's natural. And is anyone capable of courage without fear?"

IG: "I... um... no."

You: "Very well. So I'll accept your fear as a catalyst for my courage and take the audition with a new resolve."

IG: "Yeah, you're right."

==

Aaaand scene! You don't have to sound like a wannabe Socrates in your own inner dialogue, but have fun with it. If your inner guard still convinces you, then that's just a sign that you have more to explore. It might not turn around quickly, but this exercise will give you a new frame for the internal process that once paralyzed you. With a little philosophical curiosity, you can dismantle almost any assumption and redefine your mental boundaries.

WHOA THERE: FLAPPING YOUR ARMS

Whitney[21] called me in a panic.

---

[21]   Not her real name

"I think I've figured it out, or I thought I did, but it's too much," she said, catching her breath between sobs. "Can you come meet me in front of the church? Maybe I need to go to church."

This was my senior year of college, and Whitney was one of my closest friends. We had a lot of those late-night dorm room conversations about life, relationships, ethics, aesthetics, and the real meaning behind that new movie *The Matrix*. For all my pretentious insistence on philosophy, however, Whitney preferred to find her insights in literature and lived experience.

That's why I was surprised to find Whitney out on the cathedral steps with two massive door stop volumes: *The History of Western Philosophy* and *An Eastern Philosophy Anthology*. She was crying and shaking, listening to something on her Walkman. When I got to her, she put the books down, took off her headphones, and handed them to me. I immediately recognized one of my favorite songs from Ben Folds Five:

> *I pushed you 'cause I loved you guys*
> *I didn't realize*
> *That you weren't having fun*
> *And I dragged you up the stairs*
> *And I told you to fly*
> *You were flapping your arms*
> *Then you started to cry, you were too high*
> *No, too high*

In the song "Philosophy" by Ben Folds Five, the narrator appeals to his friends to embrace philosophy, even if that means questioning their beliefs, daring to reach great heights, and flapping their arms like birds (though honestly, that last part sounds more like a prank).

Still crying, Whitney told me she had been listening to this song on repeat all weekend. Something in the lyrics suddenly broke through, and she was convinced that the meaninglessness in her life was due to a shallow understanding of reality. As I had also done years ago in a moment of crisis, Whitney rushed to find books with the answers, but she was overwhelmed. She kept trying to read these great works of philosophy, getting confused, telling herself that she would never get it, and starting over, hopeless.

We were both just college kids, so what did I know? The only advice I could offer was that binging anthologies wouldn't help. While some of the most profound insights come from ancient wisdom, there are plenty of canonized writers who are so dense and impenetrable that they seem, like the inauthentic artist, to hide behind obscurity. Or maybe they're just smarter than all of us. The point was that we couldn't rush the wisdom, and some philosophical writing adds up more to dazzling logic than guidance for life.

Meanwhile, you can easily slip down the rabbit hole of "moral exhaustion," as Michael Schur calls it—the endless debates, considerations, trade-offs, wagers, and quandaries of philosophical ethics that will have you second-guessing every choice against the greater good. I highly recommend reading *How to Be Perfect* for an entertaining tour of moral exhaustion and its alternatives. For now, it's healthy to remain conscientious and consider the implications of your beliefs and actions as long as you're not full tilt into analysis paralysis.

This gets wrapped up in the existential issue that Whitney was dealing with; i.e., *what does it all mean*? Fortunately, we went to lunch and I was able to talk her down. She asked if she could get a "cheat sheet" from me, summarizing all these philosophers and what they might say about her current crisis. Her problems were her own, but not unique, which is one of the consolations of any great survey of literature, philosophy, or personal development. Still, instead of lecturing her, I listened. I asked open-ended questions, some influenced by my philosophical curiosity and some just basic clarifications. I walked her home and she took a nap ("If you don't know what you want, it's probably sleep."). I don't know if she ever picked up the big philosophical tomes again. More to her taste, I loaned her my copy of Milan Kundera's novel *The Unbearable Lightness of Being*, which explores philosophy, but with more sex and car crashes. That seemed to help.

THE BALANCING ACT: FIERCELY PRACTICAL

If this chapter inspires you to dive into the big names of philosophy, pace yourself. If the topic sounds daunting, start with YouTube for Hank Green's *Crash Course Philosophy,* or Alain de Boton's *The School of Life*. Both channels are conversational, funny, easy to follow, and favor storytelling over abstraction. I'd also recommend Tom Butler-Bowdon's *50 Philosophy Classics* for a drive-by historical survey to see what resonates. Once you build up the aptitude and patience, try tackling a single classic volume of philosophy that forces you to read slowly, pause, stare up at the ceiling every few minutes, and dive back in. Above all, acknowledging my hypocrisy for most of this chapter, explore beyond the Western canon and (*ahem*) beyond nerdy, well-meaning white guys. Seek out diverse voices who speak to philosophical traditions around the world.

Getrude Matshe, an author and speaker originally from Zimbabwe, has a powerful TEDx talk on the philosophy of ubuntu. She translates this Nguni Bantu term as meaning "I am because we are," while other scholars have described this philosophy as "the belief in a universal bond of sharing that connects all humanity."[xlvii] To illustrate ubuntu, Matshe shares stories of building libraries, saving lives, and connecting with a global force of women overcoming trauma. Her accomplishments are all from an interconnected practice that is deeply allocentric, and such a far cry of that dry cough of the ego insisting on some hollow affirmation.

No one is asking you to be a saint. As your optimal self, you can simply recognize a philosophy like ubuntu as both deeply considered and fiercely practical. Turn to philosophy to dive past the surface-level priorities that disrupt your creativity or undermine your authenticity. Then, as you follow the various threads of ancient philosophy, Stoicism, existentialism, pragmatism, utilitarianism, Buddhism… just about all of the good "isms" will invite you to worry less about what the world thinks of you, and to consider more about what you think of the world.

In a way, a journey through philosophy may transform your inner dialogue into a form of psychoanalysis. Healthy inquiry recasts the warring characters of inner guard and perceived self and gives you a healthier frame of therapist and patient. (Stoicism, again, is the source code for CBT.) The constant cognitive volleys of question and answer become less combative and more supportive. For philosopher Slavoj Zizek,[22] the point of psychoanalysis is not to dig deeper into ourselves and find the "real self," but rather to understand our behavioral patterns and redirect attention from the noise toward a higher purpose.

That said, even if you are a licensed therapist, you can't rely on your inner dialogue to override your blind spots, manically switching places between your chaise lounge and your office

---

[22]   I met Zizek around 2009 at KUOW, the radio station where I was working at the time. He autographed a kazoo for me. I still haven't figured out the symbolism there.

chair as you act out your inner therapy sessions. Philosopher Hannah Arendt put it this way:

> It is highly unlikely that we, who can know, determine, and define the natural essences of all things surrounding us, which we are not, should ever be able to do the same for ourselves—this would be like jumping over our own shadows.[23]

After exhausting yourself with a few rounds of shadow-jumping, you'll eventually have to concede that you need a coach, therapist, or both to listen and reflect back—it can be both jarring and illuminating to hear your own ideas filtered through the framework of professional support. Philosophy will also make you reckon with your treatment, connection, and reliance on those around you. After all, if you strive to be an accomplished creative, where would you be without a community?

---

[23]   Arendt's observation also gave me a brilliant idea to occupy my seven-year-old. "Let's try jumping over our own shadows!" You can burn a whole afternoon like that.

Chapter 6
Find Your Tribe—Creating Through Community

*The relations that constitute our identity are the
relations we have with others, not those we hold
between thoughts and memories in our minds.*
—Julian Baggini

I waited for the gin to kick in and curb my adrenaline. It wasn't working. I had to begin.

The floors were sticky, the stage lights blinded me, and I spent 20 seconds of my three-minute limit just trying to adjust the microphone. Still, miraculously, I managed to get through my first poetry slam unscathed. I made it to the final round and lost, but more importantly, I was suddenly surrounded by fellow poets asking me where I was from, sharing lines they liked from my performance, and encouraging me to come back.

This was March of 2001 at Seattle's Sit and Spin, an old laundromat and arcade with a performance venue in the back, a relic of the grunge era from just a few years earlier where they put up small concerts and hosted poetry slams every Wednesday night. The venue was always packed and electric. Were there umbrellas and old bikes hanging from the ceiling or was that a fever dream? Whatever this place was, it felt like a creative haven, and all it took to participate was a cover charge and a pocketful of poems.

This was just two months after I had moved to the city without a real job lined up—still leaping, still waiting for that net to appear. I had been sleeping on a mattress on the floor of a rented room for $400 a month, which I could barely afford on my temp salary. It was a step up from the halfway house, but it was still infused with that over-romanticized Bohemia of multiple 20-somethings sharing the residence with a 50-something landlord named Randall. This was a landlord who would take your dishes if you left them in the sink overnight and hide them under his bed "to teach you a lesson about personal responsibility."

With just a handful of college friends in the area, I spent my first few months in Seattle locked in that small room, sitting on the floor mattress as I wrote, memorized, and rehearsed the poems I'd perform for judgmental strangers at the Seattle Slam. By "judgmental strangers," I don't mean people being silently judgmental. Per the rules of the slam, three random people were given scorecards on a scale of 0.0 to 10 and were asked to score each poem based on... *vibes*, I guess? They weren't supposed to be experts in the form, just representatives of the crowd. Connection to the audience was everything.

I did fine in those rowdy poetry competitions, and even made it on a couple of national teams; but what really drew me in was the creative community. We met for drinks before and after the slams, formed alternative readings, traded feedback in writing circles, traveled for regional tours like small-time comedians or folk singers, got tangled in ill-advised hookups (turning the inevitable fallouts into material), sometimes competing with dual poems with our Rashomon versions of events, letting the scores decide. It was formative and free-falling and destructive and would never last.

With a couple of decades of hindsight, I'd still advise anyone intrigued by the poetry slam community to step up, with the caveat that this community represents one of the most fraught elements of creative communities: competition. In any art form, if you are vying for the same grants or auditioning for the same roles, you must get over the mindset of a "zero sum game," assuming that any peer's opportunity means one less chance you have to succeed; envy and resentment are creativity killers. While it's easier said than done, transform the charge of competition into a drive to be better than you were yesterday, not at the expense of others, but on a parallel track that still allows room for mutual support.

Yes, creative communities are messy, but consider the alternative. If you close yourself off with your art and brood in isolation, imposter syndrome will thrive in the echo chamber of your protective bubble. Solitude serves every creative to a point, but taken to the extreme, you risk self-rejection in the guise of individualism. In *The Alter Ego Effect*, Todd Herman attributes imposter syndrome to a fear of rejection from the tribe, rooted in primal instincts of survival going back millennia. "If your tribe finds out you're a fraud," writes Herman, "it triggers that primordial, 'Uh-oh, they're going to kick me out! I'm going to be caught in the wilderness alone!"

Are you an introvert? Join the club. We meet every Tuesday and stare at our shoes together. Eventually, you'll feel comfortable enough to stare at someone else's shoes. Then, one day, you'll meet a girl who writes haiku on her Converse sneakers and you'll strike up a conversation about the difference between haiku and senryu and how you've never met anyone else who gets that, but technically a haiku must mention a season, right? And so it begins.

If you truly suffer from social anxiety, start with professional support. Chances are, though, if you're a creative, then you are secretly an *ambivert*, which breaks out of the introvert/extrovert binary to lean back or lean in depending on the mood, energy, crowd, or time of day. If you start online, that's fine, just find your conspiracy of fellow ambiverts willing to emerge from your silos for an artist's circle, improv class, open mic, or Renaissance Faire.

No need to rush. If you're unsure about getting out there or cautious about how you spend your time and energy, use this Creative Community Vibe Checklist.[24]

---

[24]   Though I would advise against printing this checklist, putting it on a clipboard, and walking around the group checking it off in real time. That might land on the wrong side of creepy.

CREATIVE COMMUNITY VIBE CHECKLIST

The Question	Red Flags	Swipe Right, It's a Match
How do you feel around this group?	• Energy drain • Unsafe • Insecure	• Light • Inspired • Thought-provoking
How diverse and inclusive is the group?	• Uniformity of thought • All emulating the same styles • No diversity • Fixated on a single personality leading the group	• Diverse • Encourages competing ideas • Multiple creative styles and expressions • Group equity above any "figurehead"
How do you feel immediately after meeting up?	• Drained • Uninspired • Demotivated • Derailed	• Inspired • Energized • Motivated • Part of something bigger than yourself
How do they spend their time?	• Small talk • Complaining • Gossiping about anyone perceived as more successful	• Creating • Supportive and honest critiques • Exploring new ideas, forms of art, and techniques • Brainstorming

If you struggle to find a group that checks all the boxes, maybe it's time to start one. At minimum, find one or two creatives who inspire you and make your own community.

Steven Pressfield is adamant about the call for creative collaboration, marveling at the magic of great minds meeting:

> Hemingway in Paris gets to talk prose technique with Gertrude Stein and hang at the Closerie des Lilas with Lady Duff Twysden. Henry Miller in Montmartre can talk all night with Anais Nin and Blaise Cendrars. John Lennon in London can trade notes with Mick Jagger or turn down Eric Clapton for the gig that will go to George Harrison. None of that synergy would've happened if they'd all stayed home in Bushwick or Oak Park. It's not enough for your heart to be in the right place. Your ass has to be there too.[xlviii]

Don't let Pressfield's list of legends intimidate you, but take his call to action to heart. The good news is that you're not starting with a blank canvas. These communities have always been there, just waiting for you. Hear that music and laughter in the distance? Was that someone yelling "cannonball" before a splash? The party boat of belonging never docks or crashes ashore—you have to swim out to meet it.

THE RESONANCE ERA

Here's a selfish reason to be selfless: It will make you happier and more creative. Barbara Frederickson, one of the leading scholars in positive psychology, offers a dynamic view of social connection in her book *Love 2.0: How Our Supreme Emotion*

Affects Everything We Feel, Think, Do, and Become. Studying the trio of "shared positive emotions, biobehavioral synchrony, and mutual care," Dr. Frederickson examines the impact of "positivity resonance," or "Love 2.0."

In a series of studies with her doctoral students Lahna Catalino and Bethany Kok, Frederickson found evidence for Rochefoucauld's maxim that "love is brief, but frequently recurring." She calls these "micro moments" of positivity, expanding the definition of love beyond the reserved and rationed emotion exclusive to those closest to you. Before you shrug this thesis off as overly romantic, note that Frederickson also makes her definition of love conditional—not a passive, universal force, but the product of deliberate actions and connections that require constant renewal. If this isn't a frequently exercised muscle for you, it can sound exhausting.

Still, positivity resonance plays a key role for any creative, from intimacy to friendship to connecting with a wider audience. When you craft something to inspire, disrupt, or persuade, what are you doing if not getting inside another mind? Tell me about a song you love, a painting that haunts you, or a film that gives you chills. Think of examples from artists you've never met. In these examples, how intimate is that connection with the artist? They started a conversation without knowing how you would finish it, and some of those exchanges last a lifetime.

Let's consider, for example, what happens in your brain when you are deeply engrossed in a novel, film, podcast, or play. Frederickson describes the discoveries of Princeton neuroscientist Uri Hasson, who observed the brain activity that lights up when listening to a stranger's detailed story. They found that those who paid close attention to a pre-recorded story displayed "extensive neuronal coupling," beyond the activity of "mirror neurons" to echo isolated brain states. The best listeners even went beyond synchronizing with the storyteller's brain states. For those rapt in the one-way conversation, their brains somehow "*anticipated* [the storyteller's] brain activity by a few seconds in several cortical areas." This is science fiction-level stuff, all documented in functional Magnetic Resonance Imaging (MRI) under strict laboratory conditions.

For creatives more intuitive than I am (which is most), this likely lands as confirmation of common sense: The artist and the audience have a profound link. For those of us who overthink our craft, however, the research from Frederickson, Catalino, Kok, Hasson, and many others gives us an avalanche of scientific rationale to stop being so rational, at least in the moments of creative connection. Love may not conquer all, but *positivity resonance travels through fucking time.*[25]

The takeaway? If your relationship to your art has you in your head, it's time to get out. Get out of your head, sure, and also get out of your room, your house, your comfort zone, and discover the positivity resonance in every micro moment. To put that in a less wonky and academic way, find the current of love in your art, and let the current lead.

MINIMUM VIABLE PRACTICE: THE AUDIENCE WINDOW

Once you've established your creative peer group, they are your most reliable audience. As you extend your reach, your fans are increasingly distant, imagined, and unknown, but your peer group includes individuals who resonate with the wholehearted expression that inspired you at the start. Whether you're an

---

[25] Yes, technically the listener in these studies was anticipating brain states based on the likely direction of the story, but it still feels uncanny.

anonymous poet posting on message boards or Beyoncé performing to a sold-out stadium, you have a relationship with your audience. You may be obscure and abstract or open and confessional, but anywhere along that spectrum you are revealing aspects of yourself. If your inner guard convinces you to hide, you're not open enough to relate. If you're all ego, just out there begging for validation, you lose any hope of relevance or resonance. Between these extremes, where do you and your audience meet?

The Johari House (or Window)

Imagine walking into a house with four rooms. The first room is open and spacious, with windows and mirrors and an open door. You see a second room that others can freely enter and leave, but you're not allowed in room two. That's okay, because you have your own private room off to the side and no one else has access to room three. These three rooms seem to compose the entire house, but you've heard rumors of a fourth room. You've never seen it, and no one else has entered it, but based on the floor plans, you're certain there is another room—not to mention the mysterious sounds from the corner where the rest of the rooms converge.

Welcome to the Johari House. This is the term that philosopher Charles Handy applied to the original Johari Window technique developed by psychologists Joseph Luft and Harrington Ingham in 1955. The window in this model has four panes (as drawn below). It's a 2x2 matrix depicting your self-awareness, what others know about you, and what remains hidden.

	Known to Self	Unknown to Self
Known to Others	Open area	Blind spot
Unknown to Others	Façade (Hidden)	Unknown

You can see why Luft and Ingham call it the Johari Window (a celebrity couple mashup of their names, Joseph and Harrington), because the 2x2 division resembles a windowpane. It also makes sense to extend this metaphor, as Handy did, into the *Johari House*, because it feels more like something you inhabit than something you look through. At any rate, I use Johari Window and Johari House interchangeably.

In the original therapeutic practice of Luft and Ingham, you'd determine these quadrants by privately describing yourself from a selection of adjectives, and then others who know you well would independently select adjectives to describe you. More advanced versions go beyond adjectives to behaviors, degrees of effectiveness, preferences, strengths, opportunities, etc. It's similar to a modern corporate "360 review."

In my executive development work, I trained countless HR professionals on how to debrief these 360s, which were 80-page summaries for senior leaders incorporating anonymous feedback from their direct reports, peers, managers, and other stakeholders. When I sat down one-on-one to conduct a debrief, I often referenced the Johari Window to help them parse the differences between their intentions, assumptions, and how others perceived them. Some would turn the pages with dread, internalizing every data point. Others would flip through and shrug off anything they didn't agree with it. You could always recognize the most effective leaders, because they took it all in, took accountability, and resolved to do better. But those who shrugged it off? Funny, I rarely saw them again.[26]

Here's how the Johari Window results shake out into different "windows" or "rooms," and how they might apply to your relationship with your audience:

Open Area

You know it, they know it—heck, the whole town knows it. These are the adjectives and behaviors you all independently agreed on, out in the open.

Open Area with your audience: Are you open, confessional, and vulnerable with your audience? If not, is that intentional, or are you holding yourself back? Even the most abstract art or music takes on a new charge when you share a degree of transparency and let the audience tune into the same wavelength.

Blind Spot

Have you ever listened to a recording of your voice and thought, *Do I really sound like that?* Again, you can't jump over your own shadow. Your Blind Spot area includes everything others clearly see about you, or at least perceive, while you've been in the dark. Your blind spots can be either strengths or opportunities.

Blind Spot with your audience: In Chapter 1 we mentioned Derrida's notion that releasing your art is like releasing an animal into the wild. You can't control or tame it, and you can't be certain who will adopt it or who will run terrified. But if your work reaches anyone, at some point you will hear reviews that

---

[26] Sorry, that sounded ominous. I rarely saw them again because they often moved on to other companies.

surprise, delight, or upset you. How open are you to shining a light into those otherwise dark corners?

Façade/Hidden

Hey, no one needs to know about your fear of frogs or your pinwheel fetish. This is information that you know about yourself but others are unaware of. In interpersonal relationships, this becomes the information that often lingers beneath the social façade.

Façade with your audience: If a writer, musician, or any artist cuts deep, then the façade is at least one layer above the marrow. This is also the room where your inner guard keeps permanent residence and spends all day reinforcing your imposter syndrome. If you're vulnerable enough in your work, you can throw the inner guard some red meat to distract them from your real pursuit—just long enough to share an honest, unguarded moment with your audience. Then quickly get this vulnerable work out there before the guard turns around and tries to take it back.

Unknown

This is the vast unconscious that fuels creativity. It's impossible to know everything about yourself, which makes dreams and half-remembered childhoods so appealing to artists.

Unknown with your audience: As we established with the Default Mode Network, you might occasionally drift into rumination or revelation, fear or insight, depending on how much you trust yourself to explore these depths. Spilling over from the façade, your audience might discover something in your most vulnerable work that surprises both of you.

To improve your relationship with yourself, try expanding the open area, inviting feedback about your blind spots, and diving deep into the hidden area. As Richard Feynman reminds us, "The first principle is that you must not fool yourself—and you are the easiest person to fool." The more authentic you become with what you create, the more trust you'll build with your audience, and the less they'll let you fool yourself. The best audience will hold up a mirror to your vulnerability. Even when it's a cracked mirror, a funhouse mirror, or a blurred reflection in the river from a passing train, let yourself see the feedback as its own form of expression. Even when the mirror is flawed, it can be a portal between the rooms in your Johari House. Or Window. Look, it's a window in a house with a portal, okay? Now the house is on fire! Now the fire has turned into a thousand doves! Now the doves have flown away and you're just standing in an open field. What does it all mean?

Ta-dah, metaphors!

WHOA THERE: THE THIRSTY CREATIVE

> *The effort is worth it, because at last when you do connect,*
> *it is an otherworldly delight of the highest order.*
> —Elizabeth Gilbert

This morning, my seven-year-old daughter burst into my room at 6 a.m.

"Dad, it's an emergency!"

"What is it?"

"I wrote a song and you need to hear it."

She proceeded to sing her new epic ballad about a girl who is a witch and talks to unicorns so they can battle against the frog kingdom—you know, a tale as old as time.

When you were a kid, you likely had a captive audience. You expected and deserved unconditional praise for any creative effort. Then, at some point, your art received real feedback from a teacher who wasn't paid to praise you, or an audience who doesn't already know and love you and post everything you do to Facebook. Sometimes their reactions stung. Suddenly, you began to doubt if all that praise you received while growing up meant anything.

The dream? To transcend the risk. To create something so amazing that everyone will praise it, invite you to share it with more raving fans, absolve you of any work that requires spreadsheets, and canonize your place as a famous rock star, actor, sculptor, or juggler. (Wait, can you name a famous juggler? Maybe that's not a thing.) But if you take this dream to its logical end, your success would propel you to superstar status, surrounded not by fans, but by the entourage between you and the fans—surrounded by those expected to be your captive audience who offer unconditional praise. In short, this fantasy takes your relationship with feedback full circle, and it's infantilizing.

You can probably think of a few examples of talented artists who lost touch with reality, whose sanity and creativity suffered for it. At this phase, unconditional praise is toxic, because it breaks down the boundaries of honest reception. It's like hiring people to sneak into your home gym and replace your barbells with Styrofoam, and then hide the mirrors so you don't notice that your muscles have atrophied. In the short term, the thought of constant encouragement sounds comforting. But who are we kidding? What are the chances that you're currently sitting in your palatial estate, deciding if you can really trust your friends to be direct now that you're more famous than the world's most famous juggler? Let's step back for a moment and consider the stages of the emerging artist and where you currently stand.

BALANCING ACT: BETWEEN HIDING AND EXPLOITING

When emerging creatives set ambitious goals, sometimes we envision massive crowds as just this abstract, undulating mass of adulation—a surging collective of clicks and likes and downloads giving us life force as we inflate into towering titans of artistic genius. Or maybe that was just one of my recurring teenage dreams.

Short of delusions of grandeur and beyond the trope of the starving artist, what's a realistic way to build an audience and become a professional creative? In his viral 2008 essay *1,000 True Fans*, author Kevin Kelly breaks down the pragmatic path that serves a narrow audience of your most diehard followers:

> A true fan is defined as a fan that will buy anything you produce. These diehard fans will drive 200 miles to see you sing; they will buy the hardback and paperback and audible versions of your book; they will purchase your next figurine sight unseen; they will pay for the "best-of" DVD version of your free YouTube channel; they will come to your chef's table once a month. If you have roughly a thousand of true fans like this (also known as super fans), you can make a living — if you are content to make a living but not a fortune.[xlix]

As Kelly figures, with 1,000 true fans purchasing 100 dollars a year of your content, you hit six figures—again, not a fortune, but a living. Of course, Kelly's figures are just convenient and catchy round numbers, but his advice to create a niche is the same guidance you'll hear from the most successful marketers making fortunes from ideas that started small. Focusing on a niche doesn't mean that you exclusively write folk songs about fire hydrants or you only paint portraits of gas station cashiers. Still, find something both personal and universal in your work that resonates with enough people to support your creative living.

When we mention specific dollar amounts, maybe you consider these calculations shallow or a corruption of your creative vision. That's fine. But if you were drawn to a book called *The Accomplished Creative*, you'll need to establish what accomplishment looks like for you. Are you content to work in corporate advertising as your main gig while taking pottery classes at night? Would you rather embrace a modest lifestyle and sell just enough online courses to pay for rent and groceries? Or do you envision something massive, a creative effort that snowballs into a movement while also generating financial freedom?

Regardless of your long-term vision, it helps to look at the map of your creative journey and find that icon indicating *you are here*. The following stages of creative development are not always chronological, and some could repeat, regress, or leapfrog from one to the other. However, based on what I've seen in myself, peers, and clients, I have found this taxonomy helpful in navigating a relationship with your audience:

Hiding: At the beginning of the journey, you are a solitary artist. You're creating something, but not sharing it with anyone. You create almost exclusively in the "Façade" room of the Johari model.

Expressing: As opposed to hiding, this stage assumes an audience of at least one, but you're just testing the waters.

Exploring: At this point, you might post your work online, go to an open mic, or present your work to a class or a small gathering.

Emerging: At the emerging stage, your audience is growing and you're finding your voice. This is where your courage becomes critical.

Connecting: At the ideal stage, you're connecting. This means the audience is truly resonating and responding to your work, and there's a sense of shared meaning.

Exploiting: At the other end of the extreme, exploiting means you're using the audience's attention just in service of the ego—you're exploiting both your own talent and the trust of the audience.

Some might call the "exploiting" stage narcissistic. This is also closely tied to our discussion of the positive feedback bubble with others protecting you from reality. But if you're worrying, *Oh no, is that me?* Then, just as we observed with imposter syndrome, the fact that you have that reflection and self-awareness means that you're probably not at that extreme "exploiting" stage. It's just a cautionary note.

Of course, there are a thousand gradients of expression, risk, exposure, success, and outreach between each of these high-level stages. Consider each to be a milestone or a landmark along your creative path. Where would you say you are? If you asked a close friend, what would they say?

Really? Hmm. Okay, right. Sounds like your close friend is dealing with a lot. How about… no, no, I get it. I just meant to ask what they would say about your place along the creative path, but if you need to vent about how they're always leaning on you in times of crisis, I'm here to listen. No, it's fine, I'm just a book, but go ahead…

Wow. I can't believe you put up with that. You're a great friend! Seriously, they are lucky to have you.[27]

---

[27]   See? Starting a conversation.

Chapter 7
A Stupid Walk for Your Stupid Mental Health

If you had half an hour of exercise this morning, you're in the right frame of mind to sit still and focus on this paragraph, and your brain is far more equipped to remember it.
–John J. Ratey

The annoying thing about taking a stupid walk for my stupid mental health ... is that it works.
–John Green

"Mariana, do you want to go for a walk?"

"No! Go away!" My six-year-old daughter barely looks up from her iPad, where she walks hundreds of virtual miles every day, usually accompanied by a rainbow sloth or chased by a homicidal pig.

"Oh, you sound grumpy. But you always feel better when we go for a walk."

"Never! Be gone!"

Cut to 10 minutes later: Mariana and my nine-year-old, Julieta, are running their fingers along the cherry blossoms and giggling. We take the path past the neighborhood marsh and find the hidden trail to a small stream. The bridge over the stream is gone, but it's only three feet across, so the girls dare me to jump. I take a running leap.

Recently, Mariana saw two Miyazaki movies, and suddenly every neighborhood walk becomes her epic adventure, communing with the tree spirits and confronting invisible guardians to a forbidden realm. She conquers the shadows and lets us continue to the duck pond, where the girls practice their quacking dialects and swear that the ducks can understand. "Look, that one is talking back!"

This entire adventure takes maybe 20 minutes, but it transforms our day. In this case, I was also documenting the whole thing for an early-2022 TikTok trend called #stupidwalkchallenge, aka, "A stupid walk for my stupid mental health." As I write this in late 2022, the trend is ancient history, but it marks the zeitgeist of mid-pandemic malaise just after Omicron surged, when many of us were entering a whole new dimension of stir crazy. And guess what? According to leading physicians and psychologists, apparently you don't need a social media hook to invest in physical activity and mental clarity.

According to my Gen Z translator, calling the walk "stupid" here doesn't mean that it's a stupid idea, though in some circles any concerted effort warrants an eye roll. A friend once explained that her boyfriend doesn't work out "because he's a hipster." I guess sloth has street cred? "A stupid walk for my stupid mental health" is brilliant marketing, because it turns that hipster indifference against itself, as if you're saying, "Ugh, Okay, I'll do it," and then quickly realizing that you feel better and your blood is pumping and your brain is lighting up with possibility. *Dang it, brain! Now you're going to get me addicted to exercise.*

Walking is the great adventure, the first meditation, a
practice of heartiness and soul primary to humankind.
Walking is the exact balance between spirit and humility.

–Gary Snyder

Tolstoy, Descartes, Kafka, Hobbes, Einstein, Beethoven, Asimov, Freud, Hawthorne, Dickens, and Tchaikovsky walk into a bar. This isn't the set up for a joke. According to Mason Currey in *Daily Rituals: How Artists Work,* each of those artists and thinkers was known for walking rituals. I imagine that they each walked into a bar at some point, if only to ask for directions. For each of these geniuses, Currey notes how their regular walks broke up their routines and often led to creative breakthroughs.

You don't have to emulate Thoreau and spend four hours a day walking through the woods. Even "a brisk twenty-minute walk can dramatically alter consciousness," reports Julia Cameron. Like many thinkers and creatives, Cameron sees walking as a moving meditation and saturation in nature. If you can find a tree-lined path, says bio mechanist Katy Bowman, you can also benefit from *Shinrin-yoku,* or "forest bathing:"

> Heavily researched in Japan, forest-bathing has been shown to promote lower concentrations of cortisol, lower pulse rate and blood pressure, and a reduction of 'technostress,' as measured by a reduction in cerebral activity ... We aren't responding to the trees per se, but rather undergoing an invisible interaction with phytoncides—active chemical substances given off by plants.[1]

While "reduction in cerebral activity" may not sound conducive for creative breakthroughs, the relaxation response is more likely to relax your buzzing brain, bringing activity down from beta waves to the chill repose of alpha waves—meaning that forest bathing is in the same neurobiological neighborhood as meditation.

I almost insisted that a forest would be the best place to hurl your body through space, but I bet the ocean would have something to say about that.

The landscape is indifferent. Just start exploring! If you're feeling stuck in your creative grind, step outside and get moving, preferably past some trees or waves. Breathe in some of those sweet, sweet phytoncides, or bask in the negative ions that splash in with the tides. Dig your toes in the sand and yell at some whales. I dare you not to rush back home bubbling with new ideas.

THE WHOLE HOUSE SHAKES

> *We do not wish to escape life but to find life, to use our minds in fresh, experimental ways, to flex our emotions, to enjoy, to learn, to add depth to our days.*
> –Robert McKee

Do I stop with a stupid walk? I have so many floating boxes to check that don't require a body, or they just need the typing parts to cooperate with the thinking parts, and each stabilizing muscle or smooth flex of involuntary respiration are just supporting characters. But screw that. I get home and keep moving with a stupid sauna, stupid cold plunge, stupid variable resistance training and gamified planks and elliptical and trampoline and punching and kicking the heavy bag until the whole house shakes. Later, I might drive to jiu jitsu, where a stranger is just a friend you haven't strangled yet.

Before my heart rate settles I'm back at my desk, typing this sentence. At dusk I can hear neighbor kids whooshing and thumping on the teeter totter, yelling back and forth:

"Body!" *(Thump)*
"Mind!" *(Whoosh)*
"Body!" *(Thump)*
"Mind!" *(...)*
(...)
(...)
(...)
(Crickets chirping, radio towers buzzing, boots snapping twigs as a search party sweeps flashlights through the trees.)

A week later, the kid hitches a ride home on a passing satellite.

==

If your creative work is dancing or acting or any crafted movement, then embodiment is part of your practice. For those of us too often caught in our heads, we sometimes have to force the momentum or risk becoming untethered. Sometimes, this means attunement in meditation, and sometimes it means getting up and getting vigorous.

Did you know *hope molecules* were a thing? In a 2016 issue of the scientific journal *Physical Therapy*, researchers Cristy Phillips and Ahmad Salehi evaluated the genomic effects of the hormones pumping through your veins during exercise.[li] They must have both come back from a vigorous run before writing this paper, because they couldn't conjure a less giddy term than "hope molecules." Health psychologist Kelly McGonigal also writes about these findings in *The Joy of Movement*, and she reassures us that the brain-boosting effects of exercise are accessible to anyone:

> Anything that keeps you moving and increases your heart rate is enough to trigger nature's reward for not giving up. There's no objective measure of performance you must achieve, no pace or distance you need to reach, that determines whether you experience an exercise-induced euphoria. You just have to do something that is moderately difficult for you and stick with it for at least twenty minutes. That's because the runner's high isn't a running high. It's a persistence high.

At the right threshold of persistence and rest, you may even feel a sense of perpetual movement. If this is new, you might feel flummoxed. What the hell is going on in that body-to-brain factory of aerospace parts? Here's what you're also stacking while running away from your thoughts and toward your insights:

- **Brain Derived Neurotrophic Factor (BDNF):** Prolonged exercise triggers spikes in a metabolite known as β-hydroxybutyrate, which in turn boosts BDNF, a protein that acts on your central nervous system and is found to increase cognition and reduce symptoms of depression and anxiety.[lii] Harvard psychiatrist John Ratey says that exercise "is like taking a little bit of Prozac and a little bit of Ritalin because, like the drugs, exercise elevates these neurotransmitters."

- **Norepinephrine, Dopamine, and Serotonin:** Any light Googling like "brain chemicals make feel better how" will yield several hits on this magical trio. In the right proportions, norepinephrine will get you pumped and moving, dopamine will keep you motivated, and serotonin will help modulate mood, learning, and memory. Researchers Tzu-Wei Lin and Yu-Min Kuo found that these are also the "three major monoamine neurotransmitters that are known to be modulated by exercise."[liii]

- **Endorphins:** Yep, this is the one your annoying runner friend Christa talks about while she's sitting all sweaty across from you at the Starbucks, checking her pulse and doing hamstring stretches while you slump over your pumpkin cream cheese muffin. But take heart! You don't have to get up at 5 a.m. and run a seven-mile circuit to get some of those coveted endorphins.

You just have to go far enough to be uncomfortable and maybe a bit out of breath. At some point, your brain and body recognize you're pushing yourself, and suddenly they start shilling out endogenous opioids right there on the spot.[liv] That's right, your brain has been stashing away these feel-good chemicals the whole time, which seems kind of unfair, but now you know how to bully your brain into submission, hanging it by its ankles and shaking it until the endorphins fall out.

COME ON, BRAIN!

RELEASE THE ENDORPHINS
OR THE TORTURE WILL CONTINUE!

WHOA THERE: ONE GOOD LEFT HOOK

You see that kid over there? The one in the crowded middle school hallway? No, not the towering one with the jean jacket and Megadeth t-shirt—the one he's picking up by the collar and tossing into the girls' bathroom. Right, the scrawny one with the Vision Street Wear shirt. Now that you've seen this, do you blame him, thirty years later, when he's a forty-something taking classes in Muay Thai and Brazilian jiu jitsu back-to-back? Does it figure that he has some midlife delusions of being a weekend cage fighter like some bad Kevin James movie?

I trained and competed in full-contact kickboxing as a teenager, but in my most recent martial arts aspirations, it only took one good left hook to the head and a dazed blur driving home to make me reconsider. What good are all these brain benefits of exercise if offset by a concussion?

You didn't meet me here for a personal training session or a pep talk on macros. For that, there are plenty of books, YouTube tutorials, and your cousin Dale trying to sign you up for his gym membership buddy discount. If we're looking at the body and its limits solely in service of courage and creativity, then we're tempted to measure from a biased baseline, assuming that most creatives aspire to be brains in vats. (The dancers and actors already got waivers, remember?) "Writers like being bodiless," claims Patricia Lockwood, which is more clever than true, especially for Lockwood—a dazzling writer more carnal than most. But her observation is also true, in that broken clock sense, twice a day and adjusted for Daylight Savings.

What I'm saying is pace yourself. So many tactics in psychology and personal development are trapped in the airless arena of theory, and we're fortunate in recent years to see breakthroughs in embodied therapy, regulating the central nervous system, and reintegrating the warring factions of body and mind, land and air—the teeter totter creaking and resting on a crooked alignment with the horizon.

BALANCING ACT: CUDDLE AND TAP

An occasional strained knee or wonky shoulder I can handle, which is why I'm sticking with Brazilian jiu-jitsu. Plus, plus, plus—and the tough black belts rolling on the mat won't acknowledge this—but grappling triggers a surge of oxytocin.[iv] You know, the "cuddle hormone?" Makes sense. Sure, oxytocin is also a stress hormone associated with many subtle social interactions, but those measurements of salivary peptides reconfigure the battle. These men, women, and warriors of every gender are pulling, gripping, rolling, pinning, choking, and tapping out in service of a social bond.

To *right click>merge cells* between the last chapter and this, most creatives would do well to find a community of physical practice. Kelly McGonigal borrows a term from early-20th-century French sociologist Emile Durkheim: "Collective effervescence… the euphoric self-transcendence individuals feel when they move together in ritual, prayer, or work." We can only travel so far at home alone on our basement treadmills, but with collective, ritual sweat and strain we unlock a new level of attunement. "We crave this feeling of connection," writes McGonigal, "and synchronized movement is one of the most powerful ways to experience it."

With the right perspective, ritual physical exertion is an extension of any art. With the right gym, dojo, or triathlon route, you're signing a waiver to sacrifice your limitations in service of collective gains. Courage, skill, and inspiration also thrive here. If you're not convinced, sweat through eight rounds of heavy bag work, then lay back on the mat in corpse pose until you stop heaving. Now, stand and turn around, looking at the sweat angel glistening on the vinyl mat.

What do you call that? Does it call back?

Chapter 8
Today's the Day! Unless Yesterday Was the Day, then Pretend It's Tomorrow but Today is Yesterday. Today is... a Day!

Integrity: You choose courage over comfort. You choose what is right over what is fun, fast, or easy. And you choose to practice your values rather than simply professing them.
—Brene Brown

People often tell me that motivation doesn't last, and I tell them that bathing doesn't either. That's why I recommend it daily.
—Zig Ziglar

These days, every author, influencer, or street corner preacher wants to tell you about their morning routine. Here's mine:

⇒ I wake up seven hours before I go to sleep. You heard me. My mattress is a time machine.
⇒ What time do Navy SEALS wake up? I wake up an hour before that.

⇒ As I sit up, I'm immediately in a meditative state, where I transcend consciousness for three hours.

⇒ I then reach to my bedside table and drink 64 ounces of distilled water pulled from rain that hasn't fallen yet.

⇒ By the time most people have rolled over to hit "snooze," I've already completed 72 rounds of high-impact tractor deadlift sprint mobility inversion drills, using only my body weight. And tractors.

⇒ Oh, you like to quietly read in the morning? Cute. During my workout regimen, I was also speed-reading advanced manuscripts from each of the world's leading productivity experts, which I translated into Latin while I slept.

⇒ When I'm ready for deep work, I volunteer to tutor unregulated AI bots who want to learn how humans think when their brains are running on 100% Limitless Pill smoothies and upcycled oxygen imported from the dying breaths of Everest speed climbers.

⇒ During my pomodoro break, each day I give a new TED Talk that is simulcast in 200 languages exclusively to the underground bunkers of deca-billionaires and above.

⇒ When the green light on my office pod glows, it means my two human children have finished their daily tutoring with Naval Ravikant, Marilyn Vos Savant, and the uploaded consciousness of Alan Watts (via organic hologram, as neither of my human children have ever seen a screen).

⇒ I greet my human children. Under my supervision, our Nurture Surrogate hugs each of them for 20 seconds or until their oxytocin levels spike above baseline.

⇒ With unwavering eye contact, I reveal to each human child the latest daily chapter in an epic parable that started the day they were born and will never end, a tale about a hawk following a river and the story of each fish in that current, each dragonfly in the updraft, each spark of the campfires along the riverbank, and every revelation the hawk has had in previous lives or lives to come, or lives that never come, but each incarnation carrying the same freedom of knowing no time, no expectations (and hence no disappointment), no firm replies, formal dances, avoidable accidents, corrugated sleep, or surges of cortisol at 4 a.m.—just flight, just flight, just flight.

⇒ I trademarked the phrase "Websites it feels illegal to know," so each time someone uses it on Twitter or TikTok I get 15 cents. I make a billion dollars a day.

OPRAH OPENS THE BOX

> *Every action you take is a vote for the type of person you wish to become. No single instance will transform your beliefs, but as the votes build up, so does the evidence of your new identity.*
> –James Clear, *Atomic Habits*

Okay, maybe my routine isn't quite that dialed in. But for this final chapter, I want to offer options for putting all of these unwieldy concepts into regular practice—to make them more, well, *wieldy*. Annie Dillard reminds us, "How we spend our days, of course, is how we spend our lives." She employs that rhetorical sigh, "Of course," to both acknowledge the obvious and give a sly nod to our resistance to this "course," this journey, this track laid down by past choices and a contract we don't remember signing. Creatives can't simply call these things called "days" the sum of our lives, can we? Aren't we transcendent creatures living in a parallel reality? Since when does laundry or flossing get equal weight on the ledger with a libretto or a breakthrough beat? If you let the obligations of a given day just rush over you, an over-vigilant inner guard will render you halfhearted and then tell you that you don't have the time or energy to create.

Maybe 17 years ago, my work had become repetitive and draining, and I used the last of my savings to take a trip to California. There, I met up with my friend Melanie at the Getty Museum. As we got out of the elevator, we saw a giant insect on a canvas—14 ½ x 11 ½ feet—pinned to the wall. About this installation, "Specimen (After Dürer)," the artist John Baldessari said this: "Perhaps you can project yourself into the position of the bug and imagine yourself in some other world, being pinned to the wall as a specimen."[lvi] At the time, Baldessari's description captured it: My life felt pinned down.

Then I experienced one of those bizarre synchronicities that shook me out of this self-pity and complacency. All it took was one word.

In the Getty café, Melanie and I met with her friend Marie. Immediately after meeting, Marie looked at me as if something just occurred to her, then glanced over at Melanie as if they were going to let me in on a secret.

"What's your favorite word?" Marie asked.

"Quotidian," I said without hesitation.

They looked stunned. They shared another look, then looked at me.

"Are you serious?" said Melanie. "We just had this conversation an hour before you arrived. That's Marie's favorite word!"

The other weird thing is, at that moment I wasn't sure why I said "quotidian." It was just a word that surfaced because I had recently read a footnote about it in Shakespeare's *As You Like It*. In modern use, we usually say "quotidian" to mean "daily, ordinary, or routine." But in Shakespeare's use, "quotidian" referred to a daily fever, or a passion that drove the character to extreme devotion.

I explained (or possibly mansplained) this to Melanie and Marie, who humored me enough to agree it was a cool twist on the word. Even though I had known this, it felt more like a footnote until this moment. Suddenly, the coincidence in our conversation unlocked the meaning of the obscure trivia to take on a greater significance, and I declared then and there that I would make the Shakespearean *quotidian* my daily credo; to burn with a daily fever. I mean, not like I'd spend each day woozy and hallucinating, but more akin to the wisdom of Hindu mystic Sri Ramakrishna: "Do not seek illumination unless you seek it as a man whose hair is on fire seeks a pond."

Perhaps I was assigning too much meaning to a simple coincidence, just looking for another justification for my pretentious 20-something persona to obsess over, but I took the quotidian mantra to heart. I started to rebel against structures and predictability, insistent on creating something every day. Who needs sleep schedules? Who needs routines? Why do all these bill collectors keep calling? Don't they understand that I have moved beyond the constructs of time, money, and responsibilities?

Yeah, as you might have guessed, that hypo mania wasn't entirely sustainable. In the years since, and with the pressures to mature, I've gradually become infatuated with the modern trends of daily discipline. Since my diagnosis of moderate sleep apnea 18 years ago, I have also become obsessed with optimizing anything that supports healthy energy. Each day I meditate, hydrate, and practice my Spanish so that the owl will stop yelling at me, review my goals, and strain my body until I'm slightly harder to kill. Every morning an app notification reminds me of my goals, and I dutifully swipe through and recommit.

For all our best intentions, though, there's only so much that a daily plan can sustain.

Whenever my daily plans go awry, I think of this GIF of Oprah Winfrey opening a big box in front of an excited audience. But instead of a new car, bees fly out. "Bees! Bees! Bees!" read the captions. In the looping image, bees swarm everywhere and the audience jumps up and down and screams. (As far as I know, this scene is a digital manipulation of the original Oprah clip, and my research tells me she never actually unleashed bees on her audience.)

Regardless, the doctored Oprah clip is both endlessly funny and a perfect visualization of anticipation met with chaos. That's what my days feel like sometimes. I make these brilliant plans. Then, *bees*.

Here we are back with the Apollonian order of calendars and to-do lists vs. the Dionysian chaos of instinct and freewheeling chance. Do we have to choose?

For those playing along, by now you're probably nudging your friend at the back of the class and whispering, "I bet he's going to start talking about the balancing act between structure and chaos." *Ding ding ding!* Now, smart ass, reach under your desk and find the books on our syllabus. Look at those intimidating words that jump out from each title:

◊ Habit!
◊ Willpower!
◊ Focus!
◊ Productivity!
◊ Discipline!

Do those words inspire you? Intimidate you? Make you wince, groan, roll your eyes, or roll up into a ball and hope that someone just rolls you through your day? You're not alone! Oh, now you say you want to be alone? You got it! Leaving you alone now. I'll wait here until you're ready.

> *Do I contradict myself? Very well then, I contradict*
> *myself, (I am large, I contain multitudes.)*
> –Walt Whitman

By now it's no surprise that I'm a jumble of contradictions—a disciplined creative, an improvising program manager, and a planning improviser. Rather than structure this chapter like the others by saving the balancing act for the end, you'll find the back-and-forth and the checks-and-balances weaved throughout. While I poke fun at personal development trends, I'm a sucker for these productivity systems. But instead of just recapping what you've heard before, I'll acknowledge my debts to their insights and share my takes.

More to the point, let's take a tour of what's worked for me, what the research says, and how it can all help us become "Accomplished Creatives" when we shape these tools into life-approximating days.

NO PUPPIES WERE HARMED

Perhaps you've heard Steven Covey's classic productivity parable about rocks, pebbles, and sand. In case this is a retread for you, I'll try a twist to keep it interesting:

Imagine it's your first day on the job at the FBI as a bomb diffuser person (BDP). What are they called? Doesn't matter. You're a BDP. The clock is ticking. Field teams have just scooped up a bunch of bombs and brought them to you: A few of the bombs are the size of your fist, a few are the size of a quarter, and then there are these piles of nanobot powder bombs that they just pour on your desk.

The Field Team Lead explains that you're the only BDP available at the moment, and you have three minutes to contain all of these explosives or they will level seven city blocks in every direction.

TWIST! It's too late to diffuse these puppies—er, bombs. You're not diffusing puppies, but that's how this grizzled Field Lead talks. He calls bombs puppies. Okay, pay attention, only two minutes left now! The point is, you can't diffuse, only contain. They give you the last available bomb containment unit, which is a metallic box about the size of a microwave.

You jump into action. You pour all of the nanobot sand bombs into the unit. You then pile in all of the quarter-sized bombs. Looking good so far, and now all you have to do is... oh, for the love of... the fist-sized bombs won't fit! You try to wedge and squeeze and slam the lid closed, but—

BOOM! Goodbye seven city blocks. In every direction.

Reset the simulation.

Now you get a second chance, but this is the third act of the movie and it's no longer a simulation. You're dealing with REAL METAPHORICAL BOMBS this time, got it?

Fortunately, you also just read this explanation of time management inspired by Steven Covey:

Fist-sized bombs: These represent the biggest priorities of your day. What is non-negotiable? What can't be moved? They may be personal or professional obligations, but after careful measurement, you know that these bombs would make the biggest impact if not contained. Put those puppies in first.

Quarter-sized bombs: These tasks are important, but if you had to shuffle them around and something fell through, everyone would still survive. Pour these in around the fist-sized bombs.

Nano sand bombs: These are tasks you would like to do or that you need to do eventually, but they are much more malleable than any other priority. Can you put them off a few days, maybe even a week, and nothing will explode? Great, pour those in after everything else and let the nano sand fill the crevices between the fists and quarters.

As you'll see (if your imagination was doing this right), you can now safely close the bomb containment unit with room to spare. The simple takeaway is that you put "first things first," as Covey often said. In the real world, though, how do you identify the first things? What if a quarter suddenly morphs into a fist?

Between facilitating time management courses and driving large corporate programs, I learned one thing: Human beings have a hard time prioritizing. As David Rock notes, "Prioritizing is one of the brain's most energy-hungry processes." A simple tactic, for example, is to ignore your emails in the morning until you've reviewed your task list and calendar, mentally weighed each task, and ordered them by size and importance. If you're looking at creative tasks, this might mean you write 500 words or compose a few lines of a song before responding to messages. You're "active before reactive," as the popular productivity ditty puts it. You are a creator, not a responder. Okay, I see you nodding, you're with me, you get it.

But wait—what if the day keeps getting away from you?

TIME AFTER TIMEBOXING

The only real way to waste time, to drag the minutes to
the curb, to fill the landfill with seconds, is to let your
body be a time capsule you forget to put your heart in.
—Andrea Gibson

What if I told you there was a study that ranked the top 100 productivity hacks?

Okay, cool, I'm super busy. What was number one?

Yep, I hear you. Let me share with you the story of the monk and the duckling. One day—

No, seriously, Jeremy. I don't have time for this parable bullshit. Just give me the tactic.

Okay, *sheesh*. It's timeboxing, alright? In a 2018 study of productivity techniques featured in the *Harvard Business Review*, the number one practice was timeboxing.[lvii] On the surface, this is simply the practice of assigning every task a length of time and then reserving that time on your calendar. Marc Zao-Sanders, who wrote the summary for the *Review*, notes that this is especially helpful for creative teams:

> If you know that a promotional video has to go live on a Tuesday and that the production team needs 72 hours to work on your copy edits, then you know when to place the timebox. In fact, you know where to place the timebox: it's visual, intuitive, obvious. Working hard and trying your best is sometimes not actually what's required; the alternative — getting the right thing done at the right time — is a better outcome for all.

You might also hear this referred to as "time blocking," but that sounds like an obstruction. Timeboxing is just adding shape and intention to your schedule, protecting it as much as you can. If the boxes shift, they shift. But a calendar that falls together neatly like a perfect game of Tetris helps me breathe easier, think more clearly, and focus on important creative work. Especially as a parent with a corporate job, independent clients, and a freaking book deadline (*last chapter, let's do this!*), timeboxing is the order that helps me justify the chaos. With guardrails, I know how much room I have for experimentation or error, even if... yep, my youngest just headbutted the cat. Scratch 15 minutes off the ol' timebox.

YOUR INFINITE PARALLEL DAYS

It's a truism that social media anxiety often stems from comparing how you feel inside to how others present themselves on the outside. You've heard this, you know this. You also know there's a selectivity bias in how others present themselves online or in person, while you're the only one with unfettered access to that cluttered façade room in your Johari House. Still, how easy is it to forget that you're measuring yourself against a selective reality?

When I suggest meditation, improv, working out, mindset exercises, studying philosophy, being more social, honing your skill, and every other thing that makes you think, *Oh, right, I should try that...* Let's admit that I don't do every one of these things every single day. These practices are not, to cite one of my favorite movies, *Everything Everywhere All at Once*. In that film, Michelle Yeoh's character taps into multiple dimensions and explores endless forking paths her life could have followed, or are following, or not *following* exactly, but coexisting in parallel. A simple choice to turn left or right in a hallway splits her off into different branches of reality. Several recent books and movies have explored similar themes, including Matt Haig's *The Midnight Library* and Marvel's *Doctor Strange and the Multiverse of Madness*. Sci-fi nerds will cite dozens of other precedents for parallel universe narratives going back decades, but the theme has hit a critical mass recently.

So how do storylines about quantum entanglement help you plan your day? When you're feeling overwhelmed by what you should do, it helps to stop assuming you can cruise along in multiple time streams and accomplish every aspiration just because you see others who seem to have it all together. This is not about hoping that the polished influencers are secretly miserable. It's more aligned with that quote attributed to Philo of Alexandria: "Be kind, for everyone you meet is fighting a secret battle." That person who keeps posting how amazing her kids are doing in school? She's struggling with chronic back pain but doesn't want to complain. That guy who shares mirror selfies of his six pack? First, inside he still feels like that chubby kid who got picked on in the third grade, and second, he is on his third round of anxiety meds and is terrified he might lose his job if he can't get back on track.

The same self-delusion holds for imposter syndrome when you think everyone has more skill, knowledge, and accomplishments than you. Have you noticed that you keep comparing your worst to their best? You've got a few friends who are brilliant at marketing, others who have poured 10,000 hours into writing, photography, or yodeling, and a couple of college friends who appeared on *Jeopardy!* Okay, you might even have that one friend who seems to be the violin prodigy/ultrarunner/meditation guide/perfect mom/Nobel Laureate. You don't want what she has. She's sworn to secrecy, but let's just say it required a blood oath.

Your Movable Day

Have you strapped on your skis? Let's start the slalom toward the book's conclusion by rounding the flags of each chapter in reverse order.

Consider how movement and rest fit into your day. Find your own rhythms. I start the morning with five minutes on the trampoline, but I don't go nuts with heavy lifting until the afternoon. Meanwhile, there's my standing desk, bounding up the stairs on the way to the kitchen, and pausing under the pull-up bar to get a few reps in between a meeting and a writing session.

But I've also been known to wake up at 4 a.m. and then take a 20-minute nap at 6:30 a.m. (sleep disorders prompt curious routines). No matter your superpowers, constant movement and trying to grind through fatigue with supplements and cold brew will yield diminishing returns.

You've heard of circadian rhythms, which are mapped to a 24-hour period. You know what's hip, though, are ultradian rhythms. ULTRA! Right, it sounds extreme, but researchers are now looking at how rhythmic cycles throughout the day govern energy and attention. Sociologist Christine Carter cites studies of elite violinists who practiced an average of 3.5 hours each day, not all at once, but in 60-90-minute sessions—ultradian. Dr. Carter also notes that high performers got more sleep than lower-performing peers and "Were also far more likely to take a nap between practice sessions—nearly three hours of napping a week."[lviii]

If that sounds like a stretch, then even a 10-minute meditation could be the perfect reset between your ultradian waves. Make it a timebox, and protect it as if your performance depended on it—because it does.

Your Communal Day

Do me a favor and see how many of your recent texts sound like this:

- *Did you RSVP to the thing?*
- *Are you going?*
- *Do you need a ride?*
- *Hope you don't mind—I tagged you on Facebook in that picture of you falling off the mechanical bull.*
- *Did you steal that bull?*
- *Security footage from the bar shows someone who looks like you running out the door with the mechanical bull.*
- *How would you even carry it?*

Texts like these are the sign that you're following my advice—creating a community and finding your tribe. I don't recommend improbable bull theft, but legal concerns aside, you do you!

On the other hand, are all of your latest texts more like this?

- *Thai Palace has your order!*
- *Burger Palace has your order!*
- *Sushi Emporium is cooking up something good!*
- *Your delivery driver has left your single corn dog and butterscotch milkshake "in the driveway, hidden behind the recycling bin" as instructed!*

No shame in your culinary preferences or the convenience of hand-delivered corn dogs. We're just looking for your opportunities to get out there a little more.

What's that, you're on a deadline and can't be bothered? All good! Try making the best of it, maybe by starting a new type of party where you invite all your friends over to watch you work inside a sound-proof glass box. Don't worry—you'll be wearing one of those dog cones so you're not distracted. Keep up the good work, and just know that there are warm bodies and the beating hearts of loved ones all around.

Look! They just made up a drinking game based on your word count! Keep it up!

Your Philosophical Day

Imagine waking up, ignoring your phone for the first 30 minutes of your day, and diving into a doozy like this: "There is another world, and it is this one."

Wow, pump the breaks, Paul Éluard, it's only 6 a.m. What am I supposed to do with *that*?

"To win the war for attention..." advises Cal Newport in *Deep Work*, "Say 'yes' to the subject that arouses a terrifying longing, and let the terrifying longing crowd out everything else." This sounds reminiscent of the "liberating terror" we used while discussing Sartre. That mix of terror and longing also evokes the fear you conquer through perspective and purpose. In other words, by training attention, you're training courage.

Our modern montage of productivity often looks like a software engineer wearing monstrous headphones in front of three monitors, cascades of code reflected in her eyes as she builds the next Google or Apple or a single leaf on a tree on a distant mountain in the background of the latest Zelda release. But if these creations are the output of deep work, then what is the input that helps the creative burrow her roots into the soil and stretch toward the sun?

If philosophy still doesn't resonate, then at least find some dense inspiration (besides your professional work) that slows you down and stretches your attention span. Maybe it's quantum physics, poetry, history, socioeconomics, queer theory, or literary hermeneutics. Just make it a big, dusty hardcover that a sitcom character would hold up in front of their face to look smart before peering over the cover to spy on their nemesis. Fall down the well of deep reading and find a new appreciation for fresh air when you climb back up.

Your Mindful Day

I no longer say "rest assured" to put people at ease. I want you to be vigilant, so I now say "wake disturbed."

"Will that report be ready tomorrow?"

"Wake disturbed!"

"Wow, okay. That's intense but you have my attention."

In this way, mindfulness can prime a gentle disturbance because you're always waking up. Your Default Mode Network pulses with a fresh glow when you give each moment a new exchange rate. *Always unfamiliar!*

When someone asks you if your meditation is adding up to anything, you can tell them about the Thai soccer team. In June of 2018, 12 boys and their soccer coach were exploring a cave in Thailand when they were caught in a monsoon and trapped for 10 days. When the Thai Navy SEAL team rescued the group, were the boys huddled, pacing, or panicking? No, they were meditating. In a CNBC interview, Stanford University professor Leah Weiss credited meditation for potentially saving lives by decreasing cortisol, improving oxygen efficiency, and lowering carbon dioxide emission.[lix] So the next time someone tells you meditation is "just sitting there and not doing anything," tell them this story and let them feel like a jerk for minimizing the survival of these children—not to mention the team's posture and discipline putting us all to shame.

Meanwhile, the irony of meditation is that it suits a sort of multitasking. Walking meditation is an official practice, and if you happen to pick up the mail halfway through your meditation, I won't tell anyone. The legendary mindfulness teacher Thich Nhat Hanh suggested washing the dishes as a meditative practice, to gently scrub each dish "like bathing a baby Buddha."[ix] In this way, meditation doesn't just bookmark or cleave your day, but rather recalibrates it, like sounding a soothing chime and riding the reverberations through every task, creation, and conversation.

It's like closing out every tab in your mental browser and losing nothing.

Your Improvised Day

It's Friday afternoon and I have an improv performance tonight. I'm standing at the gas pump, staring at traffic, inhaling fumes, and wondering what might happen on stage. But the thing with improv is that you can't think about what might happen, because there's nothing to plan. You just show up.

Even if you're not an improviser, this lesson is applicable to so many anticipated moments that don't arrive as planned. Improv teaches us that:

1. There is no rehearsal
2. Presence *is* the practice

Yes, we "rehearse" in improv in the sense that we meet to play games, practice genres, perform scenes, and work our creativity muscles. But as far as the real performance, in the moment and in connection with the audience, there is no rehearsal.

If I'm standing at the gas pump and worried about how to make tonight's show better, the answer is right in front of me. I feel the cold metal of the pump handle and the stained asphalt under my feet. I hear the buzz of the neon sign and the wheels of traffic splashing through puddles. Even tuning into my heart beating, the ache in my lower back, and the ringing in my ears—it all counts as fodder for the improviser.

For a moment, I can also practice the gratitude flow state:

Gas station>attendant>attendant's boots>laces>eyelets>plastic>assembly worker>assembly worker's coffee mug>ceramic>kiln>fire>the maintenance worker who sweeps away the ashes.

Then I'm back, still here and ready to create at any moment.

Your Unstoppable Day: Back to the Bullseye

> *When we sit down each day and do our work, power concentrates around us . . . we become like a magnetized rod that attracts iron filings. Ideas come. Insights accrete.*
> —Steven Pressfield, *The War of Art*

Here's another bastardization of Steven Covey with a twist: Within your reach is a circle of control—anything you can change. Beyond this radius, your voice carries across a circle of influence—what you can affect indirectly. Finally, you can see the horizon, but can't reach the edge of your circle of concern— what you think about and want to change, but stretches beyond your scope of control. Here's how you roll through your day:

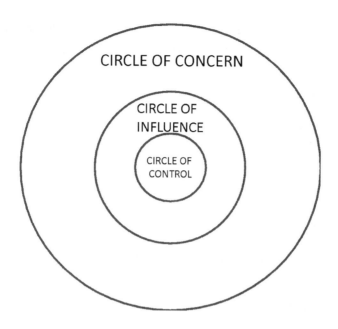

Now here's my take: Generally, the size of your timeboxes should be inversely proportional to the size of these circles. That is, your circle of control is small in proportion to your circle of concern, but channeling your energy into what you can control usually yields the best results. Will your brain get a certain kink out of doom scrolling and ruminating on everything wrong with the world? Sure, and you should be duly outraged when it fuels your service and contribution. But for now, take a few minutes each day to calibrate your circles of control, influence, and concern, and consider if you're wasting both time and energy.

You know that daunting creative project? BOOM—circle of control. Your daily habits, how you respond, the choices that you make that pump up your inspiration or leave you feeling drained—they all start with the circle of control.

If you find yourself drifting outside of what you can control, try this mantra: *Back to the bullseye.* That's the phrase I use to refocus my efforts when I'm pulled to shiny objects or uncontrollable outcomes.

- Social media feed pulling you away? *Back to the bullseye.*
- New book or course or video that isn't serving your creative vision? *Back to the bullseye.*
- Drama in your social sphere that's not about you? *Back to the bullseye.*

One coaching client added her variation as a reminder to cut out anything toxic, distracting, or out of alignment: "Block out the bullshit; back to the bullseye."

Live it. Feel it. Repeat it. Snap back into focus and feel more courageous every time. Back. To. The. Bullseye.

Your Authentic Day

> *You are under no obligation to be the same person you were five minutes ago.*
> –Alan Watts

We started this journey as an inquiry into identity, and any resolution for your day, year, or life calls for just that: Who is resolving? Who will follow through? Everyone sighs about their broken resolutions, but no one recognizes that resolutions break open like purple amethyst, all sharp and glimmering.

We've established that imposter syndrome thrives when you narrow the definition of who you are, and that carries over to your daily plans. Like Whitman, you contain multitudes. The Optimistic You makes grand plans, and the Exhausted You looks at the calendar and sighs. The Excited You RSVPs to a party, and the Introverted You gets a dopamine rush when the party is canceled. If each of these personas brandish verified check marks in your psyche as legitimately "you," then who is calling the shots?

Brian Johnson recommends starting with three aspirational identities: one for energy, one for work, and one for love (Look up Johnson's "Heroic" app for an invaluable tool to do this process each day). You could adapt Todd Herman's brilliant book *The Alter Ego Effect*, where he guides you through the process of picking a real or fictional exemplar and living as if you embodied all of those qualities. You are not "faking it until you make it," but rather tapping into that "deep inner core where a creative force resides waiting to be activated by the power of intention." For example, perhaps for energy you're The Rock, for work you're Captain Marvel, and for love you're a radiant ball of light that eats cupcakes. From there, you create a list of adjectives for each persona, and a list of general actions that you want to do each day.

Here's a quick example:

Category	Identity	Adjectives	Actions
Energy	The Rock	Courageous, Strong, Unstoppable...	Exercise, meditate, follow my nutrition protocol...
Work	Captain Marvel	Brilliant, Powerful, Creative...	Do the hard thing first, do deep work, write at least 500 words...
Love	Radiant ball of light that eats cupcakes	Compassionate, authentic, energized...	Act of kindness, celebrate someone, listen with full presence...

Here's my addition to the frameworks from Johnson and Herman: As you check off each item in the morning, imagine someone you admire greatly saying these things about you. Maybe picture them in front of an audience at the Oscars, or a commencement speech, listing these adjectives and actions as part of your bio, what you're known for. If you do this enough, any objections from your inner guard are drowned out and you can hear the whole crowd cheering. The point is not to seek external validation as your only solace, but to let your imagination populate your inner world with your singular brand of courage and optimism.

With all that, recall again that you only have this one time-line. If you intended to try this tactic or practice that tool today, but the day just got away from you, then tap into self-compassion and try again tomorrow. Living entirely in your calendar is like treating the map as the territory or trying to eat the menu. Bruce Lee's advice was simple and spartan: "Absorb what's useful and discard the rest."

For any persona you try on, always remember that you are a creative. Dive into your day not with rigid expectations but with wholehearted anticipation. If your inner guard has something to say, then invite them to pull up a seat. Is your guard sitting across from you, head-to-head, ready to battle? Or is your guard next to you, shoulder-to-shoulder, aligned with the same fears and hopes and drives all channeled toward the same brilliant end? Now your guard's inner criticism becomes a soft encouragement. Now it morphs into reconciliation, a joining of forces. The lash of self-flagellation becomes a bouquet of licorice, your *woe-is-me* radio flips to a block-rocking fight song, and the coarse acquaintance of any lesser self is flickering, faded—a tiny speck burning up in the afterburners as you approach orbit.

You're not alone.

You're here for a reason.

With the right approach, any feeling surging from within—nervous, thrilled, trembling and set free—can transform into the energy you need to finish what you started.

Acknowledgments

Oceans of gratitude to Holly Winters, Julieta Winters de Richards, Mariana Winters de Richards, Linda Sonntag, Vince Hoffart, Sarah Balka, Jessica Kazmierczak, Becky Nobach, Rick Steadman, Belinda Fu, Kahan Sudev, Bob Harpole, Rob Kosberg, Megan Maxwell, and Michael Leigh for the support, feedback, and contribution to making this book a reality.

About the Author

Jeremy Richards is a mindset and performance coach, improviser, consultant, and Senior Leadership Development Manager based in the Seattle area. His clients have included Amazon, Microsoft, Starbucks, The Gates Foundation, The Federal Reserve, and the US Army. Jeremy's writing has appeared widely, including in *Poetry*, *McSweeney's, The Huffington Post,* and on National Public Radio's *Morning Edition* and *All Things Considered.* He holds an MA in cultural studies from The University of Washington.

References

Affairs, P., & Berkeley|, U. C. (2019, March 16). Berkeley Talks transcript: Michael Pollan with Dacher Keltner on the new science of psychedelics. Berkeley News. https://news.berkeley.edu/2019/03/16/berkeley-talks-transcript-michael-pollan-dacher-keltner/

Amazon.com: Thanks a Thousand: A Gratitude Journey (Audible Audio Edition): A. J. Jacobs, A. J. Jacobs, Simon & Schuster Audio / TED: Books. (n.d.). Www.amazon.com. Retrieved July 23, 2022, from https://www.amazon.com/Thanks-Thousand-A-J-Jacobs-audiobook/dp/B07FK3QFTH/ref=sr_1_3?keywords=A.+J.+Jacobs&qid=1655674676&s=audible&sr=1-3

American Psychological Association. (2017). What Is Cognitive Behavioral Therapy? American Psychological Association. https://www.apa.org/ptsd-guideline/patients-and-families/cognitive-behavioral

Bariso, J. (2022, June 26). How Emotionally Intelligent People Use the Rule of Rewiring to Hack Their Brains and Change Their Habits. Inc.com. https://www.inc.

com/justin-bariso/emotional-intelligence-neurosci-
ence-brain-hack-how-to-change-habits.html

Chowney, P. (2016, January 13). Are you a Perfectionist or an
Optimalist? Geneva Business News | Actualités: Emploi,
RH, Économie, Entreprises, Genève, Suisse. https://www.
gbnews.ch/are-you-a-perfectionist-or-an-optimalist/

Christian, L. (2022, January 25). Gratitude Exercises to Change
Your Brain (6 Effective Practices). SoulSalt. https://
soulsalt.com/gratitude-exercises/#:~:text=Receive%20
gratitude%20by%20expressing%20it

Communication Theory. (2014, July 10). The Johari Window
Model. Communication Theory. https://www.commu-
nicationtheory.org/the-johari-window-model/

Contemporary Philosophy: Characteristics and
Currents. (n.d.). Life Persona. Retrieved August
8, 2022, from https://www.lifepersona.com/
contemporary-philosophy-characteristics-and-currents

Crowell, S. (2020, June 9). Existentialism (Stanford Encyclopedia
of Philosophy). Stanford.edu. https://plato.stanford.edu/
entries/existentialism/

Cuncic, A. (2020, May 1). What is Imposter Syndrome? Verywell
Mind. https://www.verywellmind.com/imposter-syn-
drome-and-social-anxiety-disorder-4156469

Default Mode Network - an overview | ScienceDirect Topics.
(2016). Sciencedirect.com. https://www.sciencedirect.
com/topics/neuroscience/default-mode-network

Drop The... What? (n.d.). Drop the Spoon. Retrieved July 22, 2022,
from http://www.dropthespoon.be/drop-the-spoon/#1

Everything Everywhere All At Once: 10 Of The Most Thought-Pro-
voking Quotes. (2022, May 30). ScreenRant. https://
screenrant.com/everything-everywhere-all-at-once-
most-thought-provoking-profound-quotes/

Exercise not only helps with mental health - it makes us more creative too, say scientists. (n.d.). World Economic Forum. https://www.weforum.org/agenda/2021/02/exercise-mental-health-creativity/

FeaturedNeuroscience·. (2022, June 18). The Sensations Experienced in Reading Poetry. Neuroscience News. https://neurosciencenews.com/poetry-sensation-20862/

FeaturedNeurosciencePsychology·. (2022, June 25). Impostor Syndrome: When Self-Doubt Gets the Upper Hand. Neuroscience News. https://neurosciencenews.com/impostor-syndrome-20905/

Hartt, C. (2022, April 28). The 5 Rules of Improv. https://www.backstage.com/magazine/article/easy-steps-great-improv-6513/

Huberman, A. (2021, September 27). Controlling Your Dopamine For Motivation, Focus & Satisfaction. Huberman Lab. https://hubermanlab.com/controlling-your-dopamine-for-motivation-focus-and-satisfaction/

Imposter Syndrome | Psychology Today. (2019). Psychology Today. https://www.psychologytoday.com/us/basics/imposter-syndrome

inspiration | Etymology, origin and meaning of inspiration by etymonline. (n.d.). Www.etymonline.com. Retrieved July 22, 2022, from https://www.etymonline.com/word/inspiration

Jacobs, A. M. (2015). Neurocognitive poetics: methods and models for investigating the neuronal and cognitive-affective bases of literature reception. Frontiers in Human Neuroscience, 9. https://doi.org/10.3389/fnhum.2015.00186

Kelly McGonigal on why it's so dang hard to stick to a resolution. (2014, January 8). TED Blog. https://blog.ted.com/

the-science-of-willpower-kelly-mcgonigal-on-why-its-so-dang-hard-to-stick-to-a-resolution/

Kirkpatrick's Model: Analyzing Training Effectiveness. (n.d.). Www.mindtools.com. https://www.mindtools.com/pages/article/kirkpatrick.htm#:~:text=What%20Is%20the%20Kirkpatrick%20Model

Leadem, R. (2017). 12 Leaders, Entrepreneurs and Celebrities Who Have Struggled With Imposter Syndrome. Entrepreneur. https://www.entrepreneur.com/slideshow/304273

MindTools. (2009). The Inverted-U TheoryBalancing Performance and Pressure With the Yerkes-Dodson Law. Mindtools.com. https://www.mindtools.com/pages/article/inverted-u.htm

Morning Pages | Julia Cameron Live. (n.d.). Juliacameronlive.com. https://juliacameronlive.com/basic-tools/morning-pages/

Murakami, H. (n.d.). The Running Novelist. The New Yorker. https://www.newyorker.com/magazine/2008/06/09/the-running-novelist

N. Armenta, C., M. Fritz, M., & Lyubomirsky, S. (n.d.). Functions of Positive Emotions: Gratitude as a Motivator of Self-Improvement and Positive Change. Http://Sonjalyubomirsky.com/Files/2012/09/Armenta-Fritz-Lyubomirsky-In-Press-2.Pdf.

Nittle, N. (2021, February 5). The Link Between Depression and Creativity. Verywell Mind. https://www.verywellmind.com/the-link-between-depression-and-creativity-5094193

One Day Of Thanks Is Not Enough: Gratitude is a Daily Practice. (2021, November 25). RyanHoliday.net. https://ryanholiday.net/gratitude-is-a-daily-practice/

Poets, A. of A. (n.d.). Negative Capability | Academy of American Poets. Poets.org. Retrieved August 8, 2022, from https://poets.org/glossary/negative-capability

Resources ~ RAIN: Recognize, Allow, Investigate, Nurture. (n.d.). Tara Brach. https://www.tarabrach.com/rain/

Ricoeur on the "Second Naïveté" | The Partially Examined Life Philosophy Podcast | A Philosophy Podcast and Blog. (2015, March 29). https://partiallyexaminedlife.com/2015/03/29/ricoeur-on-the-second-naivete/

Self-Confidence Versus Self-Esteem. (2015). Psychology Today. https://www.psychologytoday.com/us/blog/hide-and-seek/201510/self-confidence-versus-self-esteem

Sleiman, S. F., Henry, J., Al-Haddad, R., El Hayek, L., Abou Haidar, E., Stringer, T., Ulja, D., Karuppagounder, S. S., Holson, E. B., Ratan, R. R., Ninan, I., & Chao, M. V. (2016). Exercise promotes the expression of brain derived neurotrophic factor (BDNF) through the action of the ketone body β-hydroxybutyrate. ELife, 5. https://doi.org/10.7554/elife.15092

The Flow Model: Balancing Challenge and Skills. (n.d.). Www.mindtools.com. https://www.mindtools.com/pages/article/flow-model.htm

The Neuroscience of Gratitude and How It Affects Anxiety & Grief. (2019, April 9). PositivePsychology.com. https://positivepsychology.com/neuroscience-of-gratitude/#brain-effects

The Philosophy Of Stoicism: Five Lessons from Seneca, Musonius Rufus, Marcus Aurelius, Epictetus and Zeno of Citium. (2017, August 16). Daily Stoic. https://dailystoic.com/stoicism-five-lessons/

The Psychology of Self-Sabotage and Resistance. (2018, December 6). https://academyofideas.com/2018/12/psychology-of-self-sabotage-resistance/

This is Your Brain on Jazz: Researchers Use MRI to Study Spontaneity, Creativity - 02/26/2008. (n.d.). Www. hopkinsmedicine.org. https://www.hopkinsmedicine. org/news/media/releases/this_is_your_brain_on_jazz_ researchers_use_mri_to_study_spontaneity_creativity

Travers, M. (n.d.). Research Exposes A Shortcoming Of Mindfulness Meditation. Forbes. Retrieved August 12, 2022, from https://www.forbes.com/sites/traversmark/2022/06/28/research-exposes-a-shortcoming-of-mindfulness-meditation/

TWOWP. (2019, July 12). "I am not who you think I am" Quote. The World of Work Project. https://worldofwork.io/2019/07/who-am-i/

What's the Difference Between Ancient and Modern Stoicism? | Psychology Today. (n.d.). Www.psychologytoday. com. Retrieved August 8, 2022, from https://www.psychologytoday.com/us/blog/hide-and-seek/202207/what-s-the-difference-between-ancient-and-modern-stoicism

Wholeheartedness - transcript. (n.d.). Gratefulness.org. Retrieved July 23, 2022, from https://gratefulness.org/dw-session-1-transcript/

Endnotes

i   https://www.wikiwand.com/en/
Impostor_syndrome#cite_note-Langford19932-1

ii   https://www.frontiersin.org/articles/10.3389/fnhum.2015.00186/full#:
~:text=Poetic%20language%20plays%20with%20our%20affective%20
and%20cognitive,for%20the%20human%20brain%E2%80%9D%20
%28Turner%20and%20P%C3%B6eppel%2C%201983%29

iii   https://archive.org/details/memorycontributi00ebbiuoft/page/n5/mode/2up

iv   https://www.ncbi.nlm.nih.gov/pmc/articles/PMC4492928

v   https://www.sciencetheeearth.com/uploads/2/4/6/5/24658156/2011_
sakulku_the_impostor_phenomenon.pdf

vi   https://kajabi.com/blog/impostor-phenomenon-study

vii   What if "Imposter Syndrome" is a racist concept?
Let's talk. | Ethno-VLOGraphy, Ep. 2

viii   https://hbr.org/2021/02/stop-telling-women-they-have-imposter-syndrome

ix   https://consensus.app/details/thoughts-attempts-suppression-increase-
thought-lambert/f683ee2669205a629e98ee5601fb00d8/

x   https://www.frontiersin.org/articles/10.3389/fnhum.2012.00189/full

xi   https://thedecisionlab.com/biases/negativity-bias

xii   Charles Clay Doyle; Fred R. Shapiro; Wolfgang Mieder,
eds. (2012), *The Dictionary of Modern Proverbs*, Yale
University Press, pp. 76–77, ISBN 9780300183351

xiii   https://www.ncbi.nlm.nih.gov/pmc/articles/PMC7304239/

xiv   https://www.eurekalert.org/news-releases/955449

xv   https://www.linkedin.com/feed/update/urn:li:activity:6974398933255
000065/?src=aff-ref&trk=aff-ir_progid%3D8005_partid%3D10078_
sid%3D_adid%3D449670&clickid=SDZzC9wr-xyNTCZ3PTyDpRU
3UkDSzAQxuXCwXU0&mcid=6851962469594763264&irgwc=1

xvi   https://www.researchgate.net/publication/12688660_Unskilled_ and_Unaware_of_It_How_Difficulties_in_Recognizing_One's_ Own_Incompetence_Lead_to_Inflated_Self-Assessments

xvii   https://www.fishousepoems.org/twenty-five-aphorisms/

xviii   https://www.empoweringambitiouswomen.com/why-courage-is-more-important-than-confidence/

xix   https://www.goodreads.com/ quotes/7574274-run-towards-the-roar-the-old-people-used-to-tell

xx   https://www.theguardian.com/tv-and-radio/2021/mar/03/they-become-dangerous-tools-the-dark-side-of-personality-tests

xxi   Achor, Shawn. (2011) *The Happiness Advantage, Random House*

xxii   https://jamesclear.com/great-speeches/failures-of-kindness-by-george-saunders

xxiii   https://www.goodreads.com/en/book/show/165081

xxiv   https://harpers.org/archive/2007/02/the-ecstasy-of-influence/

xxv   https://juliacameronlive.com/basic-tools/morning-pages/

xxvi   https://books.google.com/ books?id=Jmt2PmOf4GoC&pg=PA45&lpg=PA45 &dq=%22Originality+is+not+an+attempt+to+capture+attention%22& source=bl&ots=1ZOBT2ehLU&sig=ACfU3U2qr8FjM4KvOBrAywZazvNb wBIztQ&hl=en&sa=X&ved=2ahUKEwiHhIaiw5z7AhWXATQIHbVtBn0Q 6AF6BAgtEAM#v=onepage&q=%22Originality%20is%20not%20 an%20attempt%20to%20capture%20attention%22&f=false

xxvii   http://www.improvdoc.org/bio

xxviii   https://hbr.org/2021/03/improvisation-takes-practice

xxix   https://www.hopkinsmedicine.org/news/media/releases/this_is_your_ brain_on_jazz_researchers_use_mri_to_study_spontaneity_creativity

xxx   Csikszentmihalyi, M. (1990). *Flow: The Psychology of Optimal Experience*. New York: Harper and Row

xxxi   stevenkotler.com/rabbit-hole/frequently-asked-questions-on-flow

xxxii   https://medium.com/@Vishen/the-4-rule-to-get-in-flow-84258ededec2

xxxiii   https://blogs.scientificamerican.com/beautiful-minds/ the-neuroscience-of-creativity-a-q-a-with-anna-abraham/

xxxiv   https://grateful.org/resource/gratitude-david-whyte/

xxxv   https://greatergood.berkeley.edu/article/item/why_gratitude_is_good

xxxvi   https://comedicpursuits.com/pirates-robots-ninjas/

xxxvii   https://www.journals.uchicago.edu/doi/10.1086/488943

xxxviii   https://partiallyexaminedlife.com/2015/03/29/ricoeur-on-the-second-naivete/

xxxix   https://www.nature.com/articles/nrn3916

xl   https://www.frontiersin.org/articles/10.3389/fpsyg.2014.01083/full

xli   https://psycnet.apa.org/doiLanding?doi=10.1037%2Fspa0000298

xlii https://www.forbes.com/sites/traversmark/2022/06/28/research-exposes-a-shortcoming-of-mindfulness-meditation/?sh=51f8e0d37d3f

xliii https://www.wikiwand.com/en/Lungtok_Tenpai_Nyima

xliv https://www.joriegraham.com/prose_american_poetry_intro

xlv https://dailystoic.com/you-can-do-this-you-can-do-this/

xlvi https://dailystoic.com/you-can-do-this-you-can-do-this/

xlvii https://web.archive.org/web/20130223104643/https://help.ubuntu.com/10.04/about-ubuntu/C/about-ubuntu-name.html

xlviii Pressfield, Steven. *Put Your Ass Where Your Heart Wants to Be*

xlix https://kk.org/thetechnium/1000-true-fans/

l https://www.heroic.us/optimize/plus-one/forest-bathing

li https://pubmed.ncbi.nlm.nih.gov/27037293/

lii https://www.ncbi.nlm.nih.gov/pmc/articles/PMC4915811/

liii https://www.ncbi.nlm.nih.gov/pmc/articles/PMC4061837/

liv https://pubmed.ncbi.nlm.nih.gov/6091217/

lv https://www.nature.com/articles/s41598-019-49620-0

lvi https://www.getty.edu/education/teachers/classroom_resources/curricula/contemporary_art/downloads/baldessari_specimen.pdf

lvii https://hbr.org/2018/12/how-timeboxing-works-and-why-it-will-make-you-more-productive

lviii https://www.christinecarter.com/2020/01/the-quiet-secret-to-success/

lix https://www.cnbc.com/2018/07/10/stanford-expert-explains-how-meditation-helped-the-thai-boys-survive.html?__source=twitter%7Cmain

lx https://www.stillwatermpc.org/dharma-topics/the-art-of-washing-dishes/

Made in the USA
Monee, IL
28 May 2023

34822155R00129